GREAT IDEAS
FOR SMALL
YOUTH GROUPS

Zondervan/Youth Specialties Books

GREAT IDEAS

for
Small
Youth Groups

Wayne Rice

Youth Specialties

ZONDERVAN PUBLISHING HOUSE
Grand Rapids, Michigan

Great Ideas for Small Youth Groups

Youth Specialties Books are published
by the Zondervan Publishing House
1415 Lake Drive, S.E.,
Grand Rapids, Michigan 49506

Library of Congress Cataloging in Publication Data

Rice, Wayne.
    Great ideas for small youth groups.

        1. Church group work with youth. 2. Church group
work with young adults. I. Title.
BV4447.R44   1985   259'.2   8522585
ISBN 0-310-34891-9

Edited by Pamela M. Jewell

Illustrations by Corbin Hillam

Printed in the United States of America

91   92   93   94   95 / CH / 12   11   10   9

Contents

PREFACE

The theme of this book is "It's o.k. to have a small youth group." It is dedicated to youth workers everywhere who sometimes feel discriminated against because their youth groups are small. They are not alone. Surveys indicate that four out of five youth groups in the United States would be considered "small."*

I have been a "professional" youth worker for over twenty years. My first youth group was a group of four kids, and two of those were my younger brothers. My most recent experience was with a group of about twenty young people. In between, I have been involved with all kinds of youth groups, large and small, in a variety of settings. As a Campus Life director, for example, I conducted weekly meetings numbering in excess of three hundred teenagers. I have had ample opportunity to compare the pros and cons of large and small groups and believe that although effective youth ministry can take place almost anywhere, a small youth group provides the best environment.

A few years ago, the English economist E. F. Schumacher wrote a classic book entitled *Small is Beautiful: Economics as if People Really Mattered*. He set forth a convincing set of arguments that life on this planet would be greatly enhanced if economic programs, communities, and institutions were reduced to a smaller, more "human" scale. Although I thought Schumacher's book was a bit idealistic, I found his ideas both appealing and applicable to the church.

Perhaps I should have entitled this book *Small is Beautiful: Youth Ministry as if Kids Really Mattered*. Small youth groups are not *always* beautiful; sometimes they are ugly. But small youth groups *can* be beautiful, and I hope this book will help to make this a reality in more than just cosmetic ways for your youth group.

The principles and ideas here are applicable to both high school and junior high youth groups. Except in a few instances, I do not differentiate between age groups. For the purposes

---

*From a survey of 4,724 youth workers taken in 1983 by Youth Specialties. In response to the item "Number of youth regularly attending," the results were the following: under 10—1000; 11 to 15—975; 16 to 20—885, 21 to 30—899, 31 to 40—375, 41 to 50—176, Over 50—414.

of this book, I have limited my definition of "small" to twenty-five or less; however, others will find the book applicable to their specific group sizes.

In this book, I occasionally compare small youth groups with larger ones to demonstrate that, in most cases, being large does not necessarily guarantee success or desirable results. Large youth groups do have advantages, just as small youth groups do.

I use the generic "he" to indicate both men and women.

Many of the program ideas, particularly in Part Two of this book, are reprinted with permission from the *Ideas* library published by Youth Specialties, Inc. Others were derived from a survey of more than four hundred small youth-group workers. Thanks to all of them.

Thanks also to the dozens of other youth workers from whom I have learned over the years, especially my good friends Mike Yaconelli, Tic Long, Bill McNabb, and David Grauer. Thanks to Ginny Offner for typing the manuscript, Kin Millen at Zondervan for his encouragement and patience, and Pam Jewell and Dave Lambert for their editing. Most of all, a big thank you to my wife Marci and to my children Nathan, Amber, and Corey for their support and love.

Wayne Rice

PART ONE

HOW TO WORK WITH A SMALL YOUTH GROUP

1

THE MYTH OF THE SMALL YOUTH GROUP

He seemed ashamed and embarrassed. He hung his head, stared down at his shoes and confessed, almost inaudibly, "I . . . I have a *small* youth group."

Doug was looking for advice and sympathy. For over a year Doug had worked with the youth group at his church, and despite his best efforts to attract new kids and make the group grow, it had remained small. Extremely discouraged, Doug was beginning to doubt whether he should be involved in youth ministry at all. He wasn't getting anywhere.

Doug had bought all the current books and magazines about youth ministry and attended seminars and conferences for youth workers, reading and hearing about impressive youth programs catering to hundreds of students. He began to compare his small group to the larger ones, tried to imitate them without success, and finally convinced himself that he was a failure.

Even the kids in Doug's youth group had grown tired and apathetic; young people who attended "everyone else's" youth programs were enthusiastic. The group's self-image was at an all-time low. Doug's patience was running out, and it was obvious that he was ready to give up.

Doug is not unlike many youth workers I have met who have a sincere desire to do effective youth ministry in their churches. They feel severely handicapped because their youth groups are small and don't believe that successful youth ministry is possible except in large groups. They have become victims of the "numbers game," a popular pastime in most youth ministry circles.

Anyone can play the numbers game. The only skill required is the ability to count. To win, however, you need to have a large youth group. The following conversation between two "typical" youth workers illustrates how the game is played:

Jim: "Hi, Bill. How's it going?"

Bill: "Great, Jim. We had 58 at youth group last Sunday, 41 at Bible Study, 73 at our big pizza bash, and 14 decisions for Christ last month. How's it going with you?"

Many youth workers play this game because they don't know of any other way to measure results. Good programs are well-attended programs; successful youth workers attract a lot of kids. If you don't think numbers are important, it's probably because your youth group is small.

But the numbers game can be terribly deceiving. Its emphasis on quantity over quality overlooks the fact that a youth group can be large and exciting, but unless each young person feels love and caring and is growing in an individual relationship to Christ, then youth ministry isn't happening at all. In reality, the only number that matters in youth ministry is the number one. We don't minister to groups. We minister to individuals. Small youth groups are by no means losers in the numbers game. More often than not, young people are better served in small groups than in large ones. David Elkind, in his book *All Grown Up and No Place to Go*, asserts that the only change that needs to be made in our schools to improve the quality of education and to alleviate problems like drop-outs, boredom and disruptive behavior is to reduce class size to eighteen or fewer students. "The benefits of smaller classes should be obvious," insists Elkind. Yet in many churches where the emphasis is on numerical growth, these advantages are not so obvious.

We need to identify and to affirm the benefits of smallness, both on the theoretical and on a practical level. First, however, we must refute a few of the more prevalent myths concerning small youth groups that often prevent youth workers like Doug from realizing their potential for ministry. Most of these myths probably started as true statements about particular situations. Some of them may still be true in special cases, but when applied generally, they are false and need to be unlearned by people who are serious about a youth ministry with small groups.

MYTH NUMBER 1: A BIG YOUTH GROUP IS A BETTER YOUTH GROUP.

My parents were fond of a joke, which they told frequently when I was a child: There were two children arguing heatedly over the relative superiority of their fathers.

First child: "My daddy is bigger than your daddy."

Second child: "Oh yeah? My daddy has a bigger *car* than your daddy."

First child: "So, my daddy has a bigger *house* than your daddy."

Second child: "But *my* daddy has a bigger *mortgage* on his house than *your* daddy!"

Like these two children, we all have made the assumption at one time or another that "bigger" means better. This tendency has been called "the colossus complex"—a misguided conviction that big things are always better than small things, that quality can be measured by quantity, and that success can be equated with size.

This myth is difficult for us to unlearn because we have become so conditioned by much of

American life. Words like colossal, gigantic, huge, king-sized, and extra-large *sound* impressive and inspiring. Even hamburgers sound more delicious when they have names like "Big Mac," "Whopper," or "Jumbo Jack."

Big things are status symbols: big cars, big diamond rings, big houses, big bank accounts, big offices. In our culture, quantity and size have become visible and concrete ways to measure success and quality. We assume that the most "successful" people drive the biggest cars, live in the biggest houses, and draw the biggest salaries.

Where does this value system come from? It's certainly not the value system of Christianity: Jesus taught that little is much and the meek will inherit the earth. Jesus could have had multitudes of followers wherever He went, but He chose instead to spend the bulk of His time with a small group of twelve. The values of the kingdom of God stand in stark contrast to the "colossus complex."

It's unfortunate, then, that this secular preoccupation with numbers hasn't been stopped at the front door of the Christian church. Instead, the church has only fostered this myth in more ways than most of us would care to admit.

The most successful pastors are those with the biggest churches in the biggest cities. And similarly, the most admired youth workers are usually those with the biggest youth groups. Many churches have converted their Sunday morning services from times of worship and community into programs of entertainment designed to attract large audiences, either in person or in front of television sets. A glance at the church page of many newspapers displays an incredible array of Christian celebrities, musicians, jugglers, athletes, side-show freaks, contests, prizes, and other gimmicks, intended to lure crowds into the church. Every year a list of the "ten largest Sunday schools" is published in magazines and books so that these award-winning churches might be congratulated, admired, and emulated.

In Scripture, however, the church is often compared to a family. We are all brothers and sisters in Christ. Extending that analogy a bit further, it would be correct to say that a large family is not necessarily better than a small family. Just a lot noisier.

MYTH NUMBER 2: NOTHING WORKS WITH A SMALL YOUTH GROUP.

This myth is derived from the previous one. If you make the assumption that the bigger a youth group is, the better it is; then it naturally follows that the smaller a youth group is, the more likely it is to be a failure. There are many youth workers who are defeated from the start because they don't believe that anything works with a small youth group.

Several years ago I participated in a local gathering of youth workers where the leader asked everyone to get into small groups of five or six to share ideas. My group included a young man named Jerry who was a volunteer youth sponsor at his church. Jerry was the first to speak.

"Our young people meet every week for a breakfast Bible study and prayer on Thursday morning, just before they go to school," he began. "And then on Saturday they spend the afternoon doing household chores and yard work for shut-ins and elderly people who live near the church." You could tell from the way Jerry spoke that he was both proud and excited about the youth program at his church.

"We plan at least two social activities per month for our young people," he continued, "like a swim party or a trip to the beach, a movie with pizza afterward, or a kite-flying day. Our kids love it. And, of course, that doesn't include our winter retreat and summer camp.

"This year," he went on, "we're planning to take our young people to a small mission in Mexico for a week-long work camp. Last November a hurricane destroyed the school building there, and we hope to help rebuild it. Now our kids are involved in several fund-raising projects to help with their expenses and supplies. They're really excited about going."

As Jerry continued to portray the youth ministry at his church, the other youth workers in our group were feeling uncomfortable. Although everyone was impressed, they also were somewhat intimidated, if not outright jealous. Most of us were struggling with small youth groups. We were certain, based on what we were hearing, that Jerry must have a large and active youth group.

Inevitably someone popped the question.

"How many kids do you have in your youth group?"

Without a moment's hesitation, Jerry answered, "Two."

Two? I was just as surprised by Jerry's answer as anyone in our group. I had assumed, as had the others, that Jerry had been blessed with a large youth group, bursting at the seams with kids. How else could his enthusiasm and success be explained?

I learned a lesson that day. Here was a youth worker who was pouring his time, a great deal of effort, and a lot of love into the lives of two kids, who were extremely fortunate to have someone like Jerry who disregarded the smallness of their number in ministering to them. I discovered from Jerry's example that smallness does not handicap successful youth ministry. Jerry was probably far more successful than many youth workers with big groups.

Naturally there are limitations when working with a small youth group as well as a large group. Many activities and opportunities for ministry are impossible with a large youth group but are ideal for a small one, and vice versa. Most importantly, many activities can be attempted successfully regardless of the group's size.

MYTH NUMBER 3: IF A YOUTH GROUP IS SMALL, THEN SOMETHING MUST BE WRONG.

There is an ancient belief that when calamity strikes, it is because you have committed some corresponding sin for which you are being punished. In the same way, there are those who believe that a small youth group is the inevitable result of a youth program with serious problems or no youth program at all.

This, of course, is not necessarily true. It *might* be true. Something could be wrong, but chances are that's not the case. There are many reasons why a youth group might be small, most of which have nothing to do with the quality of youth ministry. Here are some examples:

1. Small church membership. Small churches typically have small youth groups. It would be highly unusual for a small church to have an exceptionally large youth group. Furthermore, small churches are more plentiful than large churches. It's estimated that over sixty percent of the churches in the major Protestant denominations of the United States have a membership of less than two hundred people. Almost all of these churches have small youth groups.

2. The demographics of the church. Perhaps the church is composed primarily of young couples and singles. Presently I am a member of a church like that. It's a mission church that was started only three years ago and is made up almost entirely of young families. We have a large nursery and children's department, but hardly any teen-agers. In light of this, it would be wrong for our church to worry about its lack of a big youth program; all we need to do is wait a few years.

Other churches may have the opposite problem. They may be an older, established church with a large percentage of elderly people. Again, the result may be a small youth group simply because there are few teen-agers among the membership of the church.

3. The demographics of the community. In some areas the population is getting older or younger, moving away or changing its ethnic complexion. Often these considerations will have a dramatic effect on a church's ability to attract young people.

4. Choice. Some youth workers may decide to emphasize quality of ministry over quantity, choosing a style of ministry that is best suited to a smaller group. A deliberate choice to limit the size of the group is an acceptable option. Jesus Himself limited the number of His disciples.

5. Limitations. There may be a limited amount of space, money, or leadership in the church. There are many churches that are not equipped to handle large groups. If it's impossible for a church to provide the resources and leadership required for a large youth group, then it would certainly be best for that group to remain small.

6. History. Some youth workers *inherit* small youth groups; they begin youth work in churches that have *never* had much of a youth group. While this situation may lend itself to rapid improvement and potential growth, there is still nothing "wrong" with a small youth group. It provides a wonderful opportunity for ministry.

These are legitimate reasons for a youth group's being small. But smallness does not need an apology, a cure, or correction. It's expected and healthy.

On the other hand, it is very possible that a small youth group might be the result of negative factors such as a lack of leadership, a lack of congregational concern, a lack of outreach, or a lack of spiritual life. These conditions need to be corrected for the group to function at all, much less be effective.

MYTH NUMBER 4: SMALL YOUTH GROUPS ARE INSIGNIFICANT.

Most people would like to make an impact on the world—to do something with their lives that will make a difference. Unfortunately, many people believe the only way you can actually accomplish anything of importance is to do it in large groups.

This myth reminds me of one of my favorite Bible stories. God wanted Gideon to lead his people against a heavily-armed Midionite army (Judges 7), so Gideon drafted thirty-two thousand men who were ready and willing to fight. But God told Gideon that thirty-two thousand was far too many. Gideon, therefore, reduced his army by twenty-two thousand, leaving ten thousand, but God again informed Gideon that he had too many men. Gideon continued to trim his army until finally only three hundred were left, a mere one percent of the original group. But it was this small group that God used in a dramatic way to defeat the enemy.

Scripture is abundant with similar models for us to consider. Over and over again, we see God using small groups, even solitary individuals, to accomplish incredible feats. Perhaps the most well-known of all is the small group of disciples to whom Jesus ministered for three years. They literally turned the world upside down. God continues to work through small groups of people today, including small youth groups, when we allow Him.

In 1971, a small group of Quaker youth from Philadelphia, calling themselves "The Nonviolent Fleet," canoed into the oily waters of Baltimore harbor to paddle in front of a Pakistani cargo ship. The group had learned that the ship was transporting bombers, tanks, guns, and ammunition to the dictatorship in West Pakistan for use against the innocent people of East Pakistan, who were seeking freedom and a democratic form of government. The United States government, due to its longstanding treaties with Pakistan, was unwilling to halt military and economic support to the West Pakistani regime, so the small group chose to blockade the harbor to call attention to the atrocities taking place in the Pakistani war and call a halt to the arms shipments. In canoes and kayaks, they "mined the harbor with their bodies" and temporarily prevented the ship's docking. The Dock Workers Union, in sympathy with the young demonstrators, refused to load the Pakistani ships. The local and national news media picked up the story, and soon the entire nation was aware of this courageous little fleet and what they had attempted to do. Although they did not stop the ship or the war, they provided hope and encouragement for the people of East Pakistan, raised the consciousness of America, and had a significant influence on votes in the United States Congress, which subsequently stopped aid to Pakistan. "If U.S. aid had not been cut off," said one high-ranking government official, "it might have been another Viet Nam. The contribution of the Nonviolent Fleet was immensely valuable." (For more information on this inspiring story, read the book *Blockade* by Richard K. Taylor, Orbis Books, 1977.)

Your small youth group can make a real difference in this world and the next if it changes the course of even one person's life. I know that I will always be grateful to the church of my youth for providing the small youth group that gave me an opportunity to use my gifts and to discover the meaning of my faith in Christ.

MYTH NUMBER 5: THE PRIMARY OBJECTIVE OF A SMALL YOUTH GROUP IS TO GROW.

Every church wants a large, active ministry to young people. It makes a church feel younger, somehow more alive, to have lots of young people around the church. It's not uncommon, then, for a church to recruit a dynamic youth director or to enlist volunteers they hope will transform their small youth group into a large one.

That's why First Church called Dan to be their youth pastor. He was young, energetic, creative, and humorous; kids were naturally attracted to him. The church wanted Dan to "do great things" with their youth program.

After Dan arrived, he called a meeting for all the youth who were part of the group. There were only seven or eight kids in all. He told them about the exciting things that he had planned for the group, but they seemed cynical and apathetic. So Dan decided that these kids were basically losers, "nerds," and that if the youth group were going to grow, he would need to recruit some new kids.

Dan visited the high schools and the teen hangouts, met with some of the school leaders, and talked to many of the most popular kids on campus. He began to promote the "new and exciting" youth program at First Church. He booked films, speakers, and music groups, planned all kinds of interesting activities, including attendance contests with expensive prizes donated by local merchants.

Almost overnight the youth group grew to over one hundred kids who were coming every week. The church was amazed, and everyone thought Dan was great—everyone except a few nerds, that is. Most of the original group felt left out, lost in all the bustling excitement.

Dan's youth program attracted a lot of young people and attention, but the group was a failure because it did not meet needs of the young people in First Church.

When Dan left the church less than a year later, the youth program collapsed with only a few of the original group of kids remaining, now even more discouraged and frustrated than before.

Similar experiences like Dan's have occurred in churches all over America. Early in my own youth ministry career, I failed a group of young people because I was more concerned with kids who *weren't* there than those who *were*. I was more interested in numerical growth and prestige than in ministering to the young people who were a part of the church.

The purpose of a youth group, large or small, is not to entertain kids or to attract crowds, but to help young people discover the meaning of their faith, to grow in a deeper relationship with Jesus Christ. The youth group provides a place for young people within the body of Christ where they will be accepted, loved, nurtured, challenged, and called into ministry. Numerical growth will happen by itself.

Desiring growth in numbers is not bad; it is good. It's an indication of life, but it is not an end in itself.

MYTH NUMBER 6: EVERY CHURCH NEEDS A YOUTH GROUP.

Youth ministry, as we know it today, is actually a recent development in the history of the church. Fifty years ago it would have been very unusual for a church to have an organized youth group. Today, however, youth groups are quite common, and most churches consider them to be essential. But are they?

Recently at a National Youth Workers Convention in a seminar on "How to Work With a Small Youth Group," I asked participants to raise their hands if they had a youth group with fifty active members. To my surprise, quite a few did. (It has always been interesting to me that many people consider sixty or seventy people to be a "small group.")

Then I asked those people with groups of fifty or less to raise their hands. This was, of course, the largest show of hands. As I counted down the numbers—forty kids, thirty kids, twenty kids, ten kids, five kids— there were still a few hands up. "Four." A couple of hands went down. "Three." One hand remained up. "Two." His hand was still up. "One." Maybe he misunderstood my directions.

"How many do you have in your group?" I asked.

"None," he answered, smiling, "but our church sent me to this seminar because we want to get a youth group going."

He was in a small church that had no young people, except for one or two fringe kids who never came to anything. Still, this man had been elected youth director and wanted to learn how to start a youth group.

Contrary to popular belief, youth groups are neither essential nor mandatory. If there are no young people, then there is probably no need for a youth group. Even if there are two, or five, or fifteen young people in the church, there *still* may be no need for a youth group. It is entirely possible for a young person to grow up in a church and become a responsible, well-adjusted Christian adult without the benefit of a youth group.

Still, most churches insist upon organizing some kind of youth group, regardless of the number of their youth. "All good churches have youth groups," they reason, not realizing that there might be a better way to meet the needs of the young people in their church.

I've heard the story about a bride who, whenever she cooked a ham, would cut off both ends before baking it. Her husband, after noting this unusual procedure, asked her why. "Because my mother did it that way," she answered. Their curiosity aroused, they decided to ask her mother the same question. They learned it was because her mother's mother had always done it that way. Finally, they asked grandma. "Simple," she replied, "I cut off the ends so that it would fit in my pan."

Sometimes we need to ask ourselves why we do what we do in the church. As a result of the questioning, we might discover a more effective way. For example, rather than having a youth group meeting it might be best to meet individually with young people on an informal basis. Or, if the young people felt included and accepted as a part of the total church, there might not be a need to institute a "youth program."

One church, for example, decided to involve all ages in *all* of the activities and programs of the church. Worship services included contemporary music played with guitars as well as traditional hymns, and the young people were invited to participate in every service rather than in a once-a-year "Youth Sunday." The pastor's sermons were preached with the youth in mind, which actually made them more appealing to the adults. Social events and the educational programs were designed to include opportunities for everyone to participate and to learn. There simply was no need for a youth group because the young people knew they were a part of the church. Even though the young people frequently got together on their own, as friends normally do, for fellowship and other activities, the church itself was their youth group.

This, of course, may not be a practical, workable model for all churches, but neither is the traditional youth group. There are other ways to provide youth ministry than with a youth group.

2 ADVANTAGES OF A SMALL YOUTH GROUP

There's good news for people who work with small youth groups. By virtue of their size, small youth groups possess a variety of positive attributes and unique opportunities for ministry that are not always open to larger youth groups. If these advantages are acted upon, even the smallest group can be successful. Unfortunately, youth leaders of small groups sometimes view themselves and their groups as mediocre and nonviable. These negative images then become self-fulfilling prophecies.

The key to success with a small youth group is to exploit the advantages of smallness as much as possible.

ADVANTAGE #1: INTIMACY

Bob Mitchell, the president of Young Life, tells about one of his earliest experiences as a Young Life leader: At a local high school, he started a successful Young Life club, attracting a large number of teen-agers to every meeting. Many of the school leaders attended, and the club was definitely "the place to be." There was a lot of fun and enthusiastic singing, and Bob would always close with a clear presentation of the gospel.

There was one teen-age boy who came to this particular club faithfully for quite some time. He was very quiet and shy, Bob recalls, and it took several months before Bob even noticed him or paid any attention to him. One evening, this young man approached Bob after one of the meetings and announced, "Bob, I just wanted you to know that this week I decided to give my life to Christ."

"Great! Wonderful!" Bob responded. "Tell me, what brought about your decision? When did this happen?" Bob was very interested in knowing what part of the Young Life program was most responsible for reaching this young man.

"Well," the boy answered, "it was when you remembered my name."

Young people have a tremendous need to be known by adults, not only in name, but also in personal relationships. The intimacy of a small group provides a unique opportunity to get to know and care for each young person on a one-to-one basis. The small group has the potential to become something very personal in an increasingly impersonal world. This is virtually impossible with a large youth group. There are very few people who are able to build relationships that go below the surface with more than just a handful of people.

Quality relationships between adult youth workers and adolescents are the very core of authentic youth ministry. Youth work is not just organizing activities, putting on programs, teaching lessons, or keeping kids busy and off the streets. It is a relationship, a person-to-person ministry that cannot be mass-produced. In a large youth group, young people will come because of the attractiveness of the program. In a small youth group, they will come because of the individualized relationships, where genuine youth ministry can flourish.

My associate at Youth Specialties Mike Yaconelli has identified four components of an effective relational ministry to teen-agers. Each of them is enhanced considerably by the intimacy of a small youth group. The four components are these:

1. The ministry of presence. Young people need our availability—they need to know that we are there, that we are accessible. Often in a large group, youth see the adults as "too busy" with the demands of managing the program to give them individual attention. Ironically many youth workers actually "lose touch" with kids when they begin working with a large youth group. But in a small youth group, youth don't feel like they are competing for attention. A small youth group not only allows more availability but communicates that availability to the kids.

2. The ministry of nurturance. Another word for nurturance is discipleship. Spiritual nurturance cannot properly be done in large groups because it requires the kind of personal attention that can only be done individually or in small groups. Jesus understood nurturance and therefore and limited His inner circle of disciples to twelve. In the same way, a small youth group gives you the opportunity to learn the needs of each young person and to disciple him at his own pace.

3. The ministry of listening. Listening has rightly been called "the language of love." Young people desperately want adults to take time to listen to them. Listening is often difficult for busy pastors and youth workers because it seems like such a passive activity. But real listening is active, not passive, and an important part of youth work.

Occasionally I ask individuals to describe a person from their past or present who has had or is having a significant influence upon them. The most common characteristic of those who are identified is their willingness to listen. A small youth group intensifies our listening environment. It gives young people more opportunities to express themselves and allows youth workers more opportunities to be there as listeners.

4. The ministry of affirmation. A primary goal of adolescence is to develop and to establish a positive self-image. For many young people, this is a difficult task. Surveys have shown that the most important questions of teenagers are "Do you like me?" and "Am I O.K.?" This is, of course, why the peer group is so important during the adolescent years. Kids need affirmation and they can usually get it from their peers.

But they also seek acceptance from adults. Youth workers need to provide affirmation by encouraging each young person and building his self-confidence, giving him opportunities for achievement and success, and allowing him to use his gifts and abilities. A small youth group provides the opportunity to affirm each young person in a group.

The intimacy of a small youth group opens up a myriad of possibilities for authentic youth ministry. As we get to know each young person, we get to know his parents, his brothers and sisters, his friends. We can take a genuine interest in his life. We can spend time with him, giving him the kind of attention he requires.

In a large youth group, there is a danger that some young people may go unnoticed. Because there is no apparent difference, it's not easy to notice one person missing out of a large number. But when one out of ten doesn't come, everyone notices immediately, because that person represents ten per cent of the group. Each person matters a great deal in a small youth group.

In a large group there is also the danger of selective relationships. We can choose, in a large group with whom we want to have a personal relationship and whom we will avoid. Normally we tend to spend time with those who are most like us, most articulate, most outgoing, most cooperative, or best looking. Kids who don't appeal to us are ignored or given less attention than the few to whom we find it easy to relate. In a small group, however, it is impossible to ignore the presence and the importance of each one. Jesus said, "I am the good Shepherd; I know my sheep and my sheep know me" (John 10:14). Youth ministry is a shepherding ministry and requires that we also "know our sheep" on an intimate level. A small youth group makes that kind of knowing possible.

ADVANTAGE #2: COMMUNITY

A small youth group provides an ideal setting for building a Christian community. By "community," I mean the *koinonia*, the fellowship of the church that is characterized by unity and mutual, unconditional acceptance. This may seem unrealistic for a group of teen-agers, who are best known for their cliques and cruelty to each other, yet it is possible and should not be considered "optional."

When Jesus prayed for His church in John 17, His prayer was for unity. He could have prayed that the Church would grow, that it would prosper, that it would be spared persecution. Instead He prayed, "Father, make them one." When we emphasize community-building in our youth groups, we are helping to achieve Christ's desire for His people. We must make community-building a priority.

Most of the high schools in America are divided into an incredible array of social subcultures and cliques. In Southern California, for example, you can find "jocks," "preppies," "socials," "punkers," "dopers," "surfers," "brains," "low riders," "cowboys," and "nerds," just to name a few, all on the same campus. It is often a formidable task for individual young people to find their places within this highly-developed caste system.

Some young people, of course, never quite fit into any of these groups and are rejected because of their appearance, race, intelligence, socio-economic class, or for some other reason. They become "loners." Unfortunately, there are many church youth groups that are nothing more than carbon copies of the high school campus. It's a tragedy when a young person who has been rejected on the high school campus comes to a youth group at church and experiences the same kind of rejection.

A small youth group, because it is likely to be more intimate and personal than a large group, has a unique opportunity to offer acceptance and unconditional love to every young person who is a part of it. It's not something that happens automatically, but the possibility is greater in an atmosphere where everyone knows one another and constantly interrelates in some way.

The dynamics of a small town are similar to those of a small youth group. Everybody knows everyone else. People work together, see each other at social events, and get involved in the lives of one another. Small towns are not without their share of problems and feuds, of course, but there is a sense of community in a small town that cannot be duplicated in a large city.

Small youth groups often experience friction because the kids know each other too well. This is to be expected. Beneath the surface, however, there will be a deep and genuine concern for one another that is nonexistent in many large groups. We fail as youth workers when we see only the surface divisiveness and do not realize that community-building can develop even where there are differences. We should always be looking for ways to maximize unity and fellowship and minimize divisiveness.

Regardless of the size of the group, community-building always requires commitment and effort, direction and practicality. Too often, Christian community is dismissed as an abstract theological concept rather than a concrete reality. We sing, "We are one in the Spirit," but we aren't one in the way we treat each other. Similarly marriage isn't just a legal or spiritual state of being but a day-to-day reality that requires considerable effort for the marriage to be successful. There are some things one partner does that strengthen the marriage and other things that weaken it. The same is true with community-building.

One of the possible ways to strengthen Christian community within a youth group is to make certain that good communication happens. Good communication can help draw people together and make community a reality. When I worked with a small youth group for several years, community-building was a priority for me. In every meeting I always included opportunities for the young people to talk and listen to each other. I would use games, discussions, role plays, writing, anything that would help them to open up and understand each other better. It didn't take long before many of the divisions disappeared, and the group became very much like a family. Other ways to build community will be discussed later. It is helpful to remember that community is usually a by-product of being together, playing together, learning together, praying together, serving together. It doesn't just happen by having buzz groups and "fellowship" hours. It's true that a small youth group can be as cliquish and divided as a large group—but for youth workers who are concerned about community, small youth groups definitely offer a great advantage.

ADVANTAGE #3: INVOLVEMENT

One of the goals of authentic youth ministry is to get kids involved in the ministry of the church, to make "doers" of them, rather than to allow them to be spectators. In a small youth group, young people are more likely to participate and assume responsibility than in a large youth group where leadership roles may be given only to a select few.

Many of today's young people, perhaps more than previous generations, seem content to live vicariously. They watch television; they watch sports events; they watch others make music, and in some cases, they watch church. Too often the church resembles a spectator sport—a stadium full of people who are badly in need of exercise watch a handful of people who are badly in need of rest play the game. Young people cannot afford to be spectators in a world that is desperately in need of witness and service. They deny themselves the opportunities to have meaningful, firsthand learning experiences and to discover their gifts and natural abilities.

As a teenager, I was one of approximately ten kids in my church's youth group. Every time there was an election of youth group officers, I was elected. Of course, the same was true for everyone else. Every year we rotated from one job to another, but it was there I learned how to be a leader. Those opportunities ultimately had a tremendous impact on my life.

Not everyone can be a leader, but everyone can be made to feel he is an important part of the group. When a youth group is small, kids sense that their mere presence is important. When someone is absent, there is a noticeable void. In a large group, kids may choose not to attend functions simply because they know everything will go on fine without them.

Everyone can get involved in a small youth group, and each person can make a significant contribution. The entire group can take part in planning activities. Responsibilities can be divided so that everyone has something important to do. Rarely are "officers" needed in a small youth group when responsibility and leadership are shared by everyone.

Everyone can participate in discussions, asking questions and expressing his views in a small youth group because he is less intimidated by its size. In a large group of teen-agers, however, an effective discussion is almost impossible to lead because only a few outgoing youth will participate. The intimacy of a small group gets everyone involved.

Small youth groups also involve the adults of the church. When youth groups become large, most churches seek professional youth workers to run the program. A small youth group, on the other hand, remains manageable for lay people who want to serve in a meaningful way.

ADVANTAGE #4: FLEXIBILITY

One of the greatest aspects about a small youth group is flexibility and spontaneity. It's easy to manage and can be modified quickly and easily. Young people themselves are quite unpredictable and spontaneous. A small youth group allows freedom to "go with the flow." Sometimes it's necessary to shift gears and adapt to the kids' specific needs or circumstances.

Most organizations, including church youth groups, begin small and are designed to serve people. As long as the organization stays small, it exists for the people, and the people operate the organization. Unfortunately, when the organization grows, it becomes so institutionalized that it no longer serves the people. Then the people serve the organization and soon exist to maintain it.

When Mike Yaconelli and I started Youth Specialties in the late sixties, we ran the entire operation out of our garage. We worked as youth directors in churches and managed Youth Specialties "on the side." Youth Specialties was so small and easy to operate that we sometimes closed it for a week or more.

Eventually we rented an office, hired a secretary and a shipping clerk, and began to grow. We sent out mailings, published a few books, and started a magazine. It wasn't long before we hired an office manager, more secretaries, more shipping clerks, artists, and editors. We bought a computer to keep track of the entire operation, moved into larger offices, then bought bigger computers, and added more office space. Today with a large staff to manage, thousands of customers to service, conferences and seminars to do, articles to write, books and magazines to publish, and bills to pay, we no longer run Youth Specialties. Youth Specialties runs us. We can no longer be "wild and crazy guys" taking off whenever we wish. The nature of institutions requires responsibility.

The same dynamics are true of churches and church youth groups. They are personal and easily managed when they are small. They become impersonal and unwieldy when they are large. For example, let's change the date or even the *time* of a forthcoming event. With a small youth group, making a few phone calls will do. When the youth group is large, calling a meeting of the youth committee, asking the officers, getting approval by the church calendar committee, sending a bulk mailing, and announcing the change at least a month in advance will be needed. Obviously, a moment's notice is not the best way to plan youth activities, but it is one of the advantages of being small and flexible.

ADVANTAGE #5: LOGISTICS

Small youth groups also have a distinct logistical advantage over large youth groups which, like flexibility, allow them to be more creative and spontaneous. For example, it can be very difficult to move a large group of young people from one place to another unless you own a fleet of busses. But with a small youth group, one car will often suffice, which allows more frequent traveling. There's no doubt that it's easier and cheaper to organize carloads than busloads.

Similarly, a small youth group doesn't need a large, elaborate meeting place such as a youth center or meeting hall complete with a sound system. A small youth group can meet anywhere: in a home, in a restaurant, in a car or van, or in the park under a shade tree.

Time is another important logistical advantage. A small youth group gives workers more time for actual ministry. If all the time is spent in finding busses and drivers, assigning kids to busses, figuring the refreshments, organizing the program and schedules, getting supplies, sending the mailings, and collecting money, precious little time is left for ministry. Genuine youth ministry was never meant to be trapped in administration, although a certain amount is expected and required.

The simplicity of a small youth group offers other logistical advantages as well: less money, material, and supplies are needed; fewer adult youth sponsors are needed; and paperwork is reduced significantly. But perhaps the greatest logistical advantage is the individualized attention given to each young person. Some large youth groups may require a computer to keep in touch with each member. But in a small youth group, there is no substitute for consistent personal contact, whether it is done face-to-face, with a telephone call, or a handwritten note in the mail.

ADVANTAGE #6: IDENTITY

Finally, a small youth group can have a clearer sense of identity and purpose than might be possible in a large youth group. A large group often is so diversified that its goals and purposes may appear to be vague. But just as individual young people need to establish their personal identities during adolescence, so groups of young people function better when their identities are well-defined and clearly established.

Every young person in a small youth group can have a voice in the formulation of the group's goals and purposes, which is important in establishing the identity of the group. Every youth group needs to know its strengths and weaknesses and its future goals. A small youth group is better equipped to spend time discussing these issues and arriving at a group consensus by drafting a resolution, a contract, or a "statement of purpose," which can be signed by each member of the group. This endorsement gives each young person a greater sense of commitment to the group and a better understanding of his place within it. The intimacy and closeness of a small youth group enhances its identity.

Small can definitely be beautiful when its advantages are recognized and used. But it is not enough just to know that these advantages exist. If a small youth group wants to be successful, then its leaders and youth people need to build intentionally upon the strengths of smallness and act upon these special opportunities for ministry.

3 DISADVANTAGES OF A SMALL YOUTH GROUP

A small youth group is not entirely a bed of roses. There are, unfortunately, a few thorns. The purpose of this chapter is to identify some of the disadvantages that come with smallness and suggest how their negative impact can be minimized while the merits of small youth groups are emphasized. Knowing the disadvantages will help us either to avoid them or to be prepared for their impact.

DISADVANTAGE #1: LEADERSHIP

Every youth group, large or small, needs to have good leadership, both of the adult and the student variety. One of the disadvantages of a small youth group is a fewer number of people to be leaders. When the church itself is small, there will be fewer adults in the congregation who are qualified and willing to work with the youth group. When the youth group is small, there will be fewer natural leaders among the kids.

Ordinarily when there is a lack of adult leadership, the tendency is either to turn the youth program over to unqualified people or to do nothing at all. Of these two options, probably the latter is preferable. Unqualified leadership can do permanent harm, not only to the youth group itself, but to an individual's self-image, causing him to refuse to accept responsibility again. It is better to wait for the natural leaders within the group to emerge.

There are other options. One is to recruit people who are willing to fill the void and to provide them with the resources and the training they need. Books and materials are available that offer help for volunteer youth workers and student leaders. There are seminars, workshops, and conferences all over the country that expose people to good ideas and solid instruction on youth ministry. Good training takes time and a fair amount of supervision together with distributing resource materials.

J. David Stone suggests a simple but effective method for training volunteers for youth ministry that he calls the "Four Phases of Ease." Its strategy is to ease people into leadership responsibilities in an orderly fashion so that the likelihood of their success will be increased. The four phases are these:

1. I do it; you watch.
2. We do it together.
3. You do it; I'll watch and supervise.
4. You do it; I'll move on to another area.

Another way to provide leadership is to enlist several adults who are willing to equally share the responsibility for the youth program. One inherent danger of a small youth group is the tendency to think that because the group is small, it can be handled by only one person. This isn't true. Regardless of how small a youth group might be, it provides an ideal setting for the development of a team ministry—a group of willing adults who do together what none of them can do alone.

A third option is to scale down the size and scope of the youth program. It may be difficult to find leaders for a youth program that includes weekly youth group meetings, Bible studies, social events, and retreats. But it probably isn't as difficult to find people willing to get together with the young people monthly or semi-monthly.

Leadership among the youth can be developed in much the same way. A small youth group may not have an abundance of natural leaders, but each person, given the opportunity, can make a positive contribution to the group. There is really no need for officers in a small youth group. However, just as it is necessary to train adults who lack leadership skills, young people also need to be equipped and supervised so that they can succeed and discover their talents and abilities.

Recently at a youth workers' conference, I was asked by a pastor, "How can we turn our youth group over to the young people themselves so that they can have complete 'ownership' of the youth program?" My answer was simple: "You can't and you shouldn't." Every youth group needs to have committed adult leadership. Young people cannot be expected to run a youth group by themselves. They not only need adult supervision and guidance, they need the kind of adult friends and models that a church youth program can and should provide.

DISADVANTAGE #2: RESOURCES

Have you ever tried to use curriculum that began with "Divide your entire group into small groups of six"? This, of course, is a perfectly reasonable instruction unless your "entire group" has only five kids. One of the most common complaints I hear from people who work with small youth groups is, "All the books and resources for youth ministry are for big groups. None of that stuff ever works with a small youth group!"

Most resources *are* published with larger-than-average groups in mind. This is a definite disadvantage for people who work with small youth groups.

There are at least two reasons for size discrimination on the part of youth ministry publishers. The first is that most of the experienced youth workers who are asked to write youth ministry materials come from large churches and are writing from their own experience. Sometimes there is a false assumption that only youth workers with large youth groups have anything worthwhile to say.

A second reason is that large churches will buy supplies such as Sunday school curricula in large quantities. Publishers market their materials to meet the needs of the larger churches rather than those of the smaller churches, feeling that the larger numbers may be modified for smaller groups.

In chapter 1, Myth #2 says "Nothing works with a small youth group." The belief that nothing works, that all the good ideas only work with large youth groups, simply is not true. I have access to an extensive library of youth ministry resources, and none of them are labeled "for small youth groups only." Still, there are few that *cannot* be used in small groups. Likewise, according to some youth workers, there are not enough resources for large youth groups.

The key to making any resource work, regardless of the size of your youth group, is knowing how to adapt. You should never use a resource without first adapting it to fit the needs and personality of your particular youth group. Resources almost always need to be combined with something else, updated, or modified in some way. Many ideas in the second half of this book, although they were chosen especially for small groups, may need to be adapted.

Never look at ideas and resources and say, "This won't work." Instead, ask yourself, "How can I change this idea to make it work? How can I improve it?" If the idea involves large groups ask, "How can I scale it down to make it useful for my small group?" The ability to ask those kinds of questions is the ability to adapt.

DISADVANTAGE #3: DISRUPTABILITY

Disaster can strike at any time in a small youth group. If a few kids come down with the flu, it can wipe out half your youth group. If two or three families go on vacation at the same time, they may take most of your leaders with them. Disruptability is really the flip side of intimacy, community, and involvement. Because each person matters and is vitally important to the group, when someone is not present, he is missed and his absence leaves a tremendous void.

Other disruptions plague small youth groups. If a boy-girl couple who have been going together suddenly break up, it can affect the whole group. If two or three kids are angry and won't speak to each other, it can torpedo the entire program. Discipline problems in a small group also become more upsetting and create tension. A large group is able to absorb the shock of occurrences such as these without even causing a ripple in the smooth functioning of the youth program. In a small youth group these disruptions wreak havoc.

What can be done to prevent such disruptions? Unfortunately, most of the time not much can be done. Many disruptions happen unexpectedly; all anyone can do is react to them. But there are some common disruptions that can be prevented or at least prepared for. For example, you can find out in advance when families are going on vacation so that you don't plan your "big event" in the same week. You can stay in touch with group members so that you have some advance knowledge of who or what to expect at coming meetings and activities. You can plan a substitute activity "just in case" your original plan becomes inoperative due to an unexpected low turnout.

Disruptions can be frustrating and undermine the continuity, consistency, and morale of a small youth group. In spite of this, however, there are some positive side effects. In a large youth group, a disruption such as an absence, a broken relationship, or a discipline problem can go largely ignored. In a small youth group, such occurrences must be dealt with and resolved positively. When people are missing, we want to know why. If it is due to illness, we can visit them or pray for their recovery. If there is a broken relationship caused by anger, jealousy, or hurt feelings, it can be given attention and action can be taken to bring about reconciliation and healing.

Discipline problems cannot be ignored in a small group. In a large youth group, positive peer pressure may be decisive in helping to change the behavior of a disruptive young person. If someone cannot abide by the rules, they can be asked to leave. But in a small youth group, discipline problems won't go away quite so conveniently. Rather, they require direct confrontation and a lot of creative thinking to correct the situation. In a small youth group, there is more time and a greater need to deal with discipline problems immediately and compassionately. Disruptability may be the price we have to pay for the opportunity to be more involved in authentic youth ministry.

DISADVANTAGE #4: APATHY

Small youth groups tend to be a breeding place for apathy and boredom. Apathy thrives in a small youth group. Small groups don't automatically generate the kind of excitement and enthusiasm that large groups do. An example: go to a football game in a stadium with sixty thousand fans—there is something inherently exciting in the air, an expectancy as if something is going to explode. The game almost becomes secondary to the ferment of the crowd and, in some cases, the outcome of the game has more to do with the spectators than the players.

But if the same game were being played before a small group of people sprinkled among a stadium of empty seats, the game would not appear to be exciting at all. It would look rather dull and uninteresting. The same is true with youth groups.

When I had a large youth group, I acted much like a TV game host. The room was packed with kids, I would make my way to the front of the room and shout out announcements, tell jokes, make everybody laugh, get everyone to clap their hands, to jump up and down, to sing at the top of their lungs, and to have a great time. It was easy because the crowd was large and the excitement was already there.

If I were to act the exact same way in front of a *small* group, those young people would probably sit and stare as though I had lost my mind. The group dynamics simply are not the same. In a small group, things are naturally conducted in a low-key, laid-back manner; unfortunately, that can often lead to apathy.

Group dynamics, however, are not the only source of apathy. Sometimes young people have grown tired of doing the same things week after week, looking at the same faces, the same four walls. A lack of numerical growth can make a group feel stagnant and lifeless, as can a lack of direction or a lack of commitment to anything worthwhile. Often, apathy has little to do with the youth group at all but is the result of problems at home, personality changes during adolescence, or a host of other factors over which youth workers have little or no control. So some kids in your group may be active and enthusiastic, and others in the same group may seem extremely bored. If young people have become apathetic, you would be wise to find out what their apathy is saying.

How can apathy be prevented? How can it be cured? There are no simple solutions to the apathy problem, but here are nine ways to encourage participation and increase motivation with young people:

1. Find out what the needs of your young people are and try to meet them. If the kids are having their needs met, they will be interested and they will come. Use surveys, question-naires, and personal interviews to find out the issues, concerns, and problems that your kids are dealing with and then take positive steps to address those issues in the youth program.

2. Find out what your group likes to do and do it. If the kids like to sit around and talk, find ways to do that. If they like to sing, give them opportunities to sing in an atmosphere that doesn't threaten them. If they enjoy social events, service projects, or field trips, plan more for the future so they will have these to look forward to.

3. Give kids meaningful responsibility. Young people who have important jobs to do and know that others depend on them are much less likely to be passive and apathetic. Don't just put on the youth program for the kids. Get them involved, delegate responsibility, and help them to succeed.

4. Challenge each member of your group. Inspire your young people to see themselves making a difference in the world and being used by God. In the book *Ideas for Social Action*, Tony Campolo writes: "Young people are not going to be attracted to a church that tries to entertain them, but they will be attracted to a church that calls them to engage in ministry to others by helping the poor, working for racial equality, caring for the elderly, and improving life for the disadvantaged.''

5. Plan ahead and be consistent. Young people need to know that the youth program has a future and is going somewhere. By planning ahead and letting young people see what lies ahead, they will know that they have something positive to look forward to. This can be a great motivator.

6. Develop relationships. In a large youth group, kids are motivated to come because of the program; in a small youth group, relationships are the key. If community-building is given a high priority and if kids value the relationship between themselves and their youth leaders, they will come.

7. Keep communication lines open. Good communication keeps relationships alive and well. If you only have weekly or semi-monthly meetings, use the phone to stay in touch with kids. Send them postcards, visit them in their homes, get together with them casually. When a week or two goes by without personal contact, kids lose interest.

8. Use variety. Be creative. Don't do the same activity week after week. Move the location of your meeting place or take field trips. Use a variety of teaching and learning strategies and surprise your young people on occasion. Don't allow your youth program to become too predictable.

9. Serve refreshments. If it is true that "the way to a man's heart is through his stomach," then that saying goes double with teenagers. Kids love to eat. It's hard for them to be apathetic about food. With a small youth group, is isn't too difficult to find someone who is willing to provide a few inexpensive refreshments for every meeting or activity. This not only motivates kids to come, but also keeps them around afterward for discussion and fellowship.

There are many other ways to motivate young people and to keep them in the church. The quality of adult leadership, the concern and support of the church generally, the kinds of activities and their frequency all influence the interest level of the group. Fortunately, most young people are looking for something to get excited about, and it's up to youth workers to lead them to it. Apathy can be deadly and must not go unchecked.

DISADVANTAGE #5: CLIQUES

Cliques are probably the most prevalent social structure of adolescence. A clique is normally defined as a group of people who link themselves together so tightly that no one else can gain access to them. Every youth group has its share of cliques, but a small youth group is especially vulnerable.

When cliques dominate a small youth group, they can control the entire group. Some group members, if they are excluded from one or more of these inner circles, may feel so left out that they leave or refuse to participate at all. Adult youth workers are often forced to negotiate and deal with groups of young people rather than individuals when tightly formed cliques exist in the group.

Cliques most often exist because they offer their members acceptance, protection, and security. For many young people, a clique insures that they will never be left alone or unappreciated. In some ways, cliques are not all bad. Most young people would probably define positively the clique to which he belongs as "my best friends."

People who work with small youth groups, however, often have a difficult time seeing the good in cliques and spend much time and energy trying to figure out how to break them up. In reality, it can't be done. Good or bad, cliques are here to stay and are a necessary part of growing up. They must be considered a given of the adolescent years, and generally, a youth worker will have greater success working with and around them, rather than against them.

It is possible, however, to reduce the negative or destructive aspects of cliques in a small youth group. Provide, for example, as many opportunities as possible for group interaction and participation. Any time the group is doing something together—playing games, talking to each other, working on a project together—relationships between cliques are likely to improve. Group interaction also allows "outsiders" the opportunity to find close friends as well. But when kids come into a meeting in their cliques, sit together in their cliques, listen to or participate in the program in their cliques, and then leave in their cliques, there is little chance that conditions will improve. Rather than lecturing the group on the evils of cliques, involve the kids in a variety of activity-centered experiences that require communication and cooperation with each other. A small youth group makes it possible to involve everyone together in activities that may not eliminate cliques entirely, but may give everyone a chance to feel accepted and included.

DISADVANTAGE #6: MONEY

Many small youth groups feel severely handicapped because they have limited financial resources. "If only we had the money," is what those people say who mistakenly believe that successful youth programs can be purchased like a new set of clothes. It's true that youth ministry requires adequate funding, but it is a myth to think that a "poor" youth group is less able to function successfully than a "rich" group.

Still, an ample treasury does allow a youth worker to take advantage of the many excellent resources, publications, speakers, talent, and other programming aids that are available for a price. Many group activities, like camps, retreats, service projects, social events, field trips, and other outings require money and are more feasible when the youth group has strong financial backing. Large youth groups usually have this kind of support. Small youth groups, however, are unlikely to have a fair share of their church's annual budget and are left at a considerable disadvantage.

Here are a few suggestions how to improve the financial conditions of youth groups:

1. Begin now to prepare a projected budget for the coming year and submit it to your church's finance committee. It never hurts to ask.

2. Seek outside funding for your youth group from concerned adults, parents, business people, and others who would be willing to contribute monthly to help support the youth program. If you take this approach, you will undoubtedly need to get approval from your church's governing body, and you will need to maintain an accurate system of record-keeping and reporting to your supporters.

3. There are many simple but effective fund raisers that even small youth groups can do with surprising results.

4. Take advantage of the many available resources that are either free or very inexpensive. For example, your local public library has an excellent film and video library that you can use. Learn to economize.

5. Combine forces with other groups. If you want to book a film, a speaker, or music group that costs money, invite another youth group in your area to join you and to share the expense. Small groups can have the same advantages as large groups when they learn to cooperate with each other.

DISADVANTAGE #7: EXPECTATIONS

A common difficulty for many youth workers who have small youth groups is living up to the expectations of their churches. This is especially true for those who are in paid staff positions. Having a youth director on the church staff is a status symbol for some churches, and they expect this person to "work wonders" with the youth program (within a reasonable amount of time, of course) and to turn that little youth group into a big one. This is not unlike the owner of a professional baseball team who hires a new manager and fully expects to see his team in the World Series the following year. In a situation like this, there is tremendous pressure to perform and to get results. This is undoubtedly one of the reasons why the average length of tenure for youth workers in any one church is approximately a year and a half.

Even though congregations and church bodies often place unrealistic or unreasonable expectations on youth workers, their desire for tangible results is not entirely without justification. Accountability is always important, especially in the Christian church. But it is essential that the church and those who are in leadership positions share the same understanding of ministry and how results will be measured.

If you are committed to doing authentic youth ministry in a small youth group without having to produce superficial results, then it is wise to draft a job description for yourself that outlines your philosophy of ministry and what you hope to accomplish. This could be negotiated and agreed upon during the initial application process, or even after-the-fact, to clarify everyone's understanding of youth ministry.

Another way to avoid undue pressure and conflict is to inform the church of your methods and goals regularly. Request opportunities to speak to the congregation so that you can share your vision for youth ministry and report on the good things that are happening with the youth group.

Although your group may be small, it can still be visible to the church. Encourage your young people to be involved in worship and in service to the church. Likewise, get the adults of the church involved in the youth program. Meet in their homes, involve them in activities, have them come to youth group meetings, ask them to speak or to share their talents or knowledge with the kids. If you do this, people in the church will see what is happening, they will be encouraged, and they will have a better understanding of what youth ministry is all about.

4 TEN WAYS TO MAKE A SMALL YOUTH GROUP WORK

There are no easy solutions for the problems that come up with having a small youth group. Even so, the following practical tips will help you get the most from your small youth group. These are highly recommended by other youth workers with small youth groups who have learned them from experience. Remember: these are *tips*—not some magic formula ("Ten Steps to a Great Youth Group"). Nor are they necessarily listed in order of importance.

1. KEEP A POSITIVE ATTITUDE

"Our youth group is a dud."

Nothing can destroy authentic youth ministry faster than a group of young people who have developed a negative self-image and think of themselves as losers, worthless, and going nowhere. Small youth groups often are full of kids who feel defeated, discouraged, and dispirited. Why?

In many cases, young people only reflect the negative attitudes of their youth leaders. Youth workers who communicate negativism will get negativism back. We must be careful not to put our young people down because they are small in number. Sometimes it's possible to do that without even realizing it. For example, if you continually push kids to "bring their friends" so that the group will be larger, of if you repeatedly call attention to all the things you *could* do if only there were more kids, then you inadvertently communicate to the group that they are inadequate and not O.K. the way they are.

It is essential that you, as a youth group leader, set an example for your kids and keep a positive attitude about your youth group. Make an effort to encourage and compliment your young people, both individually and as a group. Make each one feel important and worthy of your time and energy. Let them know that you consider it a privilege not only to be their leader but a friend as well. Also, keep your sense of humor. A positive attitude on your part will do wonders to boost the morale of the group and to encourage each young person to become more involved and committed to the group.

2. DO SOME LONG-RANGE PLANNING

Many small youth groups are run with little or no advance planning of activities. Most often this is because there's been a frequent turnover of leaders or a lack of commitment on anyone's part. Often no one feels a need to do anything more than maintain the youth program on a week-by-week basis.

Long-range planning is just as important for small groups as it is for large groups. It communicates to young people that the group has direction and stability. Also it helps to prevent inevitable schedule conflicts, which can be disastrous for a small youth group.

Long-range planning should be done at least a year in advance, with planning sessions once every three months to keep the calendar up to date. With a small youth group, everyone can be invited to participate in the planning process. Dates should be chosen for camps, retreats, special events, and other activities. Topics for study can be selected and scheduled during the year. With this kind of advanced planning, plenty of room can still be left on the calendar for flexibility and spontaneity.

Small youth groups should establish a few traditions. An annual Christmas hayride, an all night grad party, or a Halloween "lock-in" are examples of traditions that can be repeated each year. One small youth group in the San Francisco area makes an annual 400-mile journey to Mexico during Easter vacation to make repairs on an orphanage.

One important tradition for my youth group was an annual "Great Race" (see page 164) that we held four years in a row on the same weekend. It grew in popularity from one year to the next, and we collected many incredible "Great Race" stories to share. Youth groups need a few traditions to give their group a history that is uniquely their own and to establish a feeling of continuity.

3. DON'T TRY TO COMPETE WITH THE SUPERGROUP DOWN THE STREET

There is a little-known proverb (I just wrote it!) that says, "A small group is not a large group." This proverb may not sound very profound, but there are many youth workers who sometimes forget this simple truth. You can't make a small youth group act like a large youth group. There are some things that a big group can do that a little group simply cannot do.

Group singing is a good example. Few small groups can make themselves sound like a large youth group that has several guitar-playing song leaders and a chorus of seventy or eighty enthusiastic voices singing "I've Got a River of Life Flowin' Out of Me, Splash-Splash-Splash-Splash." It's a great song, but it sounds terrible when your guitar player only knows one chord and three out of four kids can't carry a tune. Youth groups don't have to sing to be youth groups. Unless your group has an exceptional song leader and plenty of willing voices, it would probably be best to leave the singing to the big group down the street.

Keep in mind that a small group cannot do *as much* as a large youth group. Don't overplan your youth group. If your group is small, don't try to see how many activities per month you can schedule. Large youth groups can promise weekly meetings and Bible study groups, four social activities per month, service projects and field trips every weekend, monthly concerts and special events, four weekend retreats, three choir tours, and two summer camps. Young people in large youth groups can pick and choose the activities they want to attend, but those in a small youth group usually feel obligated to attend everything. Don't exhaust your kids. Usually one weekly meeting, one social event per month, and two or three retreats or overnighters per year are plenty.

Set realistic goals for your youth group. Your small youth group can accomplish significant things, but you will frustrate your young people if you set your goals so high they seem out of reach. For example, a friend in Florida, whose church is located across the street from a local high school campus, felt a burden to have his youth group minister to that high school. He and his youth group of about twenty young people committed themselves to "reach that high school campus for Christ" during the following year. They made a valiant effort to accomplish their goal by sponsoring a youth crusade and a Christian rock concert and distributing gospel tracts throughout the school. Unfortunately, they made a negligible impact and felt defeated because the goal was set so high. It would have been better to make a commitment to reach five or ten kids, even twenty, rather than the entire school. It's better to exceed your goal than to fall miserably short.

As a youth leader, you must also attempt not to feel threatened by the neighboring supergroup, which offers exciting and entertaining programs week after week. Such a group appears to be a "sheep-stealer" out to lure young people away from all the small youth groups in the area. It can be a double threat when young people in your group wonder why their group isn't like that and begin putting pressure on you to compete. Competition is not necessary. If your small youth group is building on its own strengths—relationships, community, involvement, there is no need to feel threatened by programs that have other strengths.

4. NEVER CANCEL AN ACTIVITY BECAUSE OF LOW ATTENDANCE

The young people in my youth group enjoy going on backpacking trips, so we planned an overnight backpack trip up one of our Southern California mountains with a campout at the summit. It was scheduled for Thanksgiving weekend. As the date drew near, however, it became clear that not many kids were going to be able to go. Two days before we were to leave, only three kids had signed up to go.

My first inclination was to reschedule the trip for a better weekend when most of the group could come. My reasoning was undeniably sound—we were still going to have to do the same amount of work and preparation for three kids as twenty—so why not postpone it until later. Besides, we had invited a guest speaker who was to lead our time around the evening campfire. It would definitely be better to wait until everyone could be there.

But, three kids had signed up to go. They were looking forward to the hike, and I knew they would be disappointed at the news to call it off. We went ahead with our plans and climbed the mountain with three kids and our guest speaker. We had a wonderful time. It wasn't exactly the same as it would have been with the entire group, but in many ways it was better. Those three kids felt very special, and the two days with them gave me a chance to get to know them and to minister to them in a personal way.

A frequent hazard in working with a small youth group is a low turnout for a meeting that was planned for a larger group. Some activities require a certain minimum number of people to be feasible. What do you do when the attendance drops below that required minimum? Normally, there are two options: Go ahead with the event and hope for the best or cancel it and send everybody home. But there is usually a third and better option: Go ahead with the activity but adapt it to the smaller group or go ahead with an alternative activity that might be better suited for the few who are there. For example, if only a handful of kids show up for a youth group meeting, it might be a good idea to go somewhere for ice cream sundaes and good conversation.

If you cancel an event because of low attendance, you risk communicating to those who did come that they're not worth your time. It is much better to be thankful for the faithful few and to take advantage of the opportunity to deepen your relationship with those young people in a creative way.

5. CHOOSE A MEETING SPACE THAT FITS YOUR GROUP

A small youth group has the advantage of not being limited by meeting space while a large group is limited because a large enough meeting space for the group must be found. However, small groups need meeting space that is *small* enough to fit the group. Many youth workers overlook this simple but important rule: Always meet in a room *only slightly* larger than the size of your group. A youth group of twenty should never meet in a room that is capable of holding two hundred. It makes the group feel even smaller. On the other hand, if a group of twenty meets in a room that only holds twenty-five, the group is likely to feel bigger.

Room dynamics can dramatically affect the spirit and tone of a meeting. When the room feels full, the atmosphere is one of excitement as well as intimacy. But it's difficult to feel intimate when the meeting place is so large that voices echo.

Similarly, don't set up more chairs than needed. Sometimes there is a tendency to set up too many chairs. It's better to set up more chairs as people arrive than to sit and stare at empty seats.

The casual atmosphere of a home is often an ideal setting for a small youth group. A living room naturally feels warmer and more personal than a classroom or church building. When kids are surrounded by familiar objects—sofas, plants, lamps, a fireplace—they are more likely to feel at home, to be themselves, and to participate. Homes are suitably equipped for youth meetings because there's usually a stereo for playing music before or after the meeting, a refrigerator for refreshments, and a soft, carpeted floor that makes chairs unnecessary. Homes are not without problems, of course. Crying babies, ringing telephones, unexpected guests, and intruding pets can create annoying distractions. If you do choose to meet in a home, it is wise to take such things into consideration.

Small youth groups rarely have the exclusive use of a building or rooms in the church. Normally, space is shared by several different groups. If you do have a room or building that can be used primarily for youth group activities, decorate it appropriately. You can carpet the floor inexpensively by sewing carpet samples together. You can put up posters, bulletin boards, photos of the group, and toss pillows and cushions around the floor for casual seating.

One youth group in the San Fernando Valley made good use of an old toolshed that was located on the church property. They made the necessary repairs to insure that it was safe, cleaned it, painted it, decorated it inside and out, and dubbed it "The Shack." From then on, their youth group meetings were held there and called "Pack the Shack." And they usually did.

The church growth movement has coined the term "critical mass" to refer to a certain minimum number of people required to create a feeling of warmth and excitement in any given congregation. That minimum number will vary from one church to another. If a church reaches or surpasses its "critical mass," it will feel alive and moving forward. If it falls below that "critical mass," however, it will feel dead and going nowhere. The concept is sound, but it is important to note that, in most cases, if the church meets in an auditorium that seats one thousand, "critical mass" will probably be in the neighborhood of six or seven hundred people. But if a church meets in a small auditorium that only holds a hundred, then its "critical mass" will be only sixty or seventy. The feeling of warmth and aliveness will be the same for the church of seventy or seven hundred. Similarly, in a youth group, "critical mass" can be controlled simply by choosing meeting space that is appropriate to the size of the group rather than trying to increase the size of the group to fit the existing rooms available. Ironically, the latter approach is the one most commonly taken. However, people are far more important than buildings and facilities, so we should try to adapt meeting places to fit our youth group's size.

6. COMBINE FORCES WITH OTHER YOUTH GROUPS

Every small youth group needs to establish an ongoing, cooperative relationship with at least one other youth group in the immediate vicinity. Youth groups from different churches can be valuable resources for one another by doing things together regularly. One of the tragedies of denominationalism is that in every community there are dozens of small, struggling youth groups, all with the same goals and objectives, all with the same Lord, but all with hardly any knowledge of each others' existence.

You can greatly enhance the quality, efficiency, and validity of your youth group by combining forces with other groups from time to time. The benefits are many:

1. Your young people will have the opportunity to meet and to fellowship with other Christian kids who attend the same schools they do.

2. Your young people will be exposed to other Christian traditions and experience firsthand that there can be unity in the midst of diversity.

3. It will provide a change of pace for your young people as they are given the opportunity to meet new faces.

4. It will allow you to do things together that would otherwise be impossible.

5. Your youth group will save money when you share expenses for concerts, films, special programs, social activities, transportation, and resources.

There are all kinds of activities that youth groups can do together. You can combine youth meetings, perhaps with the host group putting on the program for the visiting group. You can plan social events—swim parties, scavenger hunts, lock-ins, and banquets. You can combine to do mission or service projects or an evangelistic outreach. Camps and retreats, concerts, and field trips can also be done cooperatively with real success. If nothing else, you can challenge a neighboring youth group to a volleyball or softball game now and then.

Three youth groups in a rural Georgia community recently decided to make a formal alliance. They combined their groups into one larger youth program, which they now call "Youth Family." Although they come from three different denominations—Baptist, Methodist, and Assembly of God—they have decided to put aside their differences and to cooperate rather than compete. Their youth sponsors and staff meet jointly for planning. They combine their youth budgets into one common bank account and conduct all their youth group meetings at one location rather than three. They meet separately at their own churches for Sunday School, Bible studies, and worship, but most of their other activities are done together as a "Youth Family."

These three youth groups, with the blessings of their congregations, are demonstrating all kinds of new possibilities for ministry. They have discovered the "best of both worlds": the intimacy and community of smallness plus the high profile and excitement of a large youth group. This model may not be ideal for every community, but it does show there are some interesting options available for people who want to maximize the effectiveness of small youth group ministry.

7. PARTICIPATE IN DENOMINATIONAL AND NONDENOMINATIONAL EVENTS

Almost every denomination sponsors a variety of regional and national youth events: retreats, conferences, summer camps, mission and service opportunities, and rallies. They are often subsidized, in part or in whole, by the denomination from monies already collected from local churches, including yours. It makes good sense to take advantage of these events, especially if your group is small. It exposes kids to the larger church and helps them to see themselves as part of a larger body.

In addition, there are numerous parachurch or nondenominational organizations like Youth for Christ, Young Life, Intervarsity Christian Fellowship, Campus Crusade for Christ, Group Magazine, and Youth Specialties Ministries that sponsor outstanding events and activities for young people. Most of these organizations design programs to support and supplement local church youth ministries, rather than to compete with them. Many pastors and youth workers, however, are reluctant to promote these activities because they fear that their young people might become so involved they won't have time for their church. In most cases, local parachurch ministries like Campus Life and Young Life give kids an excellent opportunity to fellowship with other Christian kids. And they often provide high quality activities and role models that a small church cannot duplicate.

My small youth group always looked forward to attending local Christian concerts. We hardly ever missed Disneyland's big gospel music night. We went to camp every summer at Forest Home Christian Conference Center, joining dozens of other youth groups for a tremendous week of fellowship, fun, and inspiration.

Many youth groups make an annual journey to Estes Park, Colorado, for Group Magazines' Christian Youth Congress. Organizations like Teen Missions and Mountain T.O.P. sponsor mission trips and service projects all over the world. Youth Specialties Ministries conducts annual "Grow For It" seminars for high school students in major cities throughout the United States. It would be worthwhile to get on the mailing lists of organizations such as these and take advantage of what they have to offer.

8. INCORPORATE YOUR YOUNG PEOPLE INTO THE LIFE OF THE CHURCH

Kids need to be involved in the church, whether the youth group is large or small. But churches with small youth groups especially need to include its young people in all of its services, activities, and programs. Youth are not just in training to become "the church of tomorrow" but should be considered a vital part of the church today.

A small youth group by itself cannot offer young people all the opportunities they need to use their gifts and be involved with others in the church. The kids need to be able to participate with all ages in social activities, in mission projects, and in worship services. The youth can be involved with the young children in many ways—teaching them, playing with them, planning and providing activities for them. They can also be involved with the seniors of the church in much the same way—interacting with them, serving them, learning from them. As Maggie Kuhn of the Grey Panthers has said, "The only place in society where people can have a true intergenerational activity is in the church."

Sometimes older adults are reluctant to allow young people to participate in worship services because they envision their sanctuary being invaded by loud guitars, drums, balloons, and clowns running up and down the aisles. While it is true that most churches could stand a little more diversity and creativity in their worship services, such radical changes are hardly necessary. Rather than allowing the youth group only one Sunday a year to participate in worship, every service of the church needs to be planned in the light of the question, "How can we include the young people?" Teenagers can do almost everything adults can do—read Scripture, lead responsive readings, provide music, take the offering, lead singing, be ushers or greeters, and even preach. When young people know the church is *their* church and they are included and welcomed into the life of the church, a youth group's "smallness" is hardly an issue.

9. DON'T IGNORE AGE DIFFERENCES

Churches with large youth programs often have separate groups and separate leaders for their junior highers, senior highers, and college-age youth. This group arrangement enables the church to meet the specific developmental needs of each age group more effectively.

But small youth groups rarely have this option. If there are only five or six kids in the group—junior highers, senior highers, and all—it tends to be self-defeating to divide up into even smaller groups.

Still, there are significant differences between younger and older adolescents that can create potential problems and should not be overlooked. For example, junior highers and senior highers do not normally coexist well in the same group. The reasons for this incompatibility are rather basic. Physically, they don't look the same, and since junior highers are smaller and much less developed, they feel inferior, and the high schoolers feel superior. Of course, there may not be a great deal of difference between a fast-developing eighth grader and a slow-developing ninth or tenth grader, but if you have a slow-developing seventh grader in the same group with a mature twelfth grader, one is physically a child and one is physically an adult.

Intellectually, many junior highers have not made the shift from concrete to abstract thinking, while most high schoolers are proficient, which makes communication very difficult. Socially, junior highers are usually more cliquish, less independent, and less secure. Emotionally, junior highers can be unpredictable and inconsistent in their behavior. They embarrass easily, yet they often have a need to show off and attract attention. High school students will regard this kind of behavior as silly and childish. Such differences can create difficult moments in a youth group.

For these reasons, it is usually beneficial to have at least two separate youth programs— junior high and senior high. Some youth workers with small groups say, "Our group is too small for both a junior high and senior high group." But that is often precisely the reason why the group is small. If the group is not adequately meeting the needs of the kids or there are frequent conflicts, the group remains small. Sometimes dividing the group allows each group to thrive. Junior highers, as well as senior highers, feel more comfortable participating with kids their own age and are more likely to invite their friends.

Sometimes different age groups can combine in one group. If the leadership is good and the kids are agreeable, the "one big happy family" approach can work. However, it is important to know the potential hazards and to have a plan for minimizing their negative impact. For example, in a group that includes both junior and senior highers, a younger teen may view an older teen as either: (1) an important friend, advocate and model, making him feel big, or (2) an oppressor and an intimidator, making him feel small. The senior highers can be directed and encouraged to assume the former role and to care for their younger "brothers and sisters."

In a combined group, the leadership needs to be shared by both the high schoolers and the junior highers. The tendency in a mixed group is for all the leadership to go to the older youth, but junior highers are capable of handling some of the responsibility. They need to know they are an important part of the group.

Communication in such a diverse group can be difficult. In teaching/learning situations, you should make the subject matter relevant on two or three different levels. While it's possible to relate effectively to both groups at once, it is wise to consider the needs of all the youth and, if necessary, provide a number of learning options that kids can choose according to their level of understanding. For example, introduce the topic to the whole group then divide into smaller groups with adult leaders for further discussion.

This awareness of age level differences has a bearing on other activities as well. For example, recreation should include games that all can play, regardless of physical size or strength. Special events and social events should be designed for everyone, though it is wise to plan a few "extra" events for junior highers only or senior highers only. The rule is to be sensitive to everyone's needs.

Youth ministry rarely is dependent upon a particular method to be successful. Programs and structures are only tools. The key to success is always the people involved. With good leadership—caring adults who are sensitive to the needs of kids—practically any configuration of age groups will work.

10. DEVELOP A PHILOSOPHY OF YOUTH MINISTRY INDEPENDENT OF SIZE

Effective youth ministry can happen in a small youth group only if you adopt a philosophy that is independent of the size of your youth group. It is not enough simply to "not worry" about being small or to keep reminding yourself that being small isn't all that bad. You need to choose a well-defined and philosophy of youth ministry that gives you a sense of purpose, direction, and confidence whether your group is large or small.

If your philosophy is oriented toward programming, then the size of your group is a very important consideration. You need a lot of kids to come to all your meetings, programs, and activities. A small youth group can be very frustrating if you base your philosophy on programs.

Another philosophy that is dependent on numbers is the "superstar" approach. The church brings in the sharp, talented youth worker whose job is to impress the young people and to attract a lot of new kids to the youth program. Youth ministry built on the superstar model needs numerical growth to validate itself.

Here are some examples of other approaches to youth ministry that don't require large numbers to be workable.

1. The Relational Model: This philosophy of youth ministry is centered around relationships established between adult youth workers and the young people of the church. As adults get to know kids in a personal way and build friendships with them, opportunities for ministry open up naturally.

2. The Community Model: In this philosophy priority is given to building positive relationships between the young people themselves. A group that emphasizes community is always looking for ways to strengthen Christian unity and to provide a place where everyone feels loved and accepted.

3. The Discipleship Model: This approach emphasizes each young person's walk with Christ. The youth worker's role is to help young people grow in the faith, to add content to their faith, to learn how to think, to question, and to discover for themselves what it really means to follow Christ.

4. The Service Model: This philosophy of ministry puts a premium on the importance of learning the Christian faith by experience—by being "doers" of the Word, by putting faith into practice. They try to emulate Christ's compassion for the poor and needy, frequently becoming involved in mission and service projects.

5. The Worship Model: This approach gives significance to the place of worship and devotion in the life of the Christian. It provides young people with good opportunities for meaningful corporate worship, and also encourages personal devotions, prayer, and Bible study.

These are, of course, oversimplified, but they do illustrate the point that there are a variety of quality approaches to youth ministry that are independent of size considerations. It's not important whether you adopt one of these philosophies, develop your own philosophy, or combine them all into one. What does matter is that *you* define your objectives and goals.

Often it's important to communicate your philosophy of ministry to parents, the church's governing body, the congregation, or the young people themselves. Verbalizing helps you to develop a philosophy that you've thought through, feel committed to, and are comfortable with. Only then will you be able to forget about numbers and get on with authentic youth ministry.

5 SMALL YOUTH GROUPS CAN GROW

It's normal for living things to grow. Growth is a sure sign that life is present. Usually it doesn't happen all at once, but rather over an extended period of time, and sometimes in spurts. Growth—in plants, animals, and people—is a result of health. Good health naturally and spontaneously leads to good growth. Rarely will any living thing *try* to grow. But it will try to stay healthy.

I have a thirteen-year-old son who is beginning to grow so fast that it's hard to keep him in clothes. In spite of the expense, I'm very thankful that he is growing, which is a good indication that he is normal and healthy. Had I given him special vitamins and growth pills to artificially stimulate his body, his growth would not be a good indicator of his health—in fact, it could be misleading. Although he might have the appearance of a normal, growing boy, his health might be in jeopardy.

Likewise, growth in the church should not be forced. Much attention has been given in recent years to church growth; some attention has been good, some bad. Church growth has itself become a sophisticated science, incorporating the latest advances in research and computer technology into a proliferation of books, conferences, and organizations. The message is clear: Any church can grow if it wants to grow and is willing to pay the price for growth. Call in the experts, go to the seminars, order the software, use all the right techniques, and your church will grow, guaranteed or your money back.

But is this really the kind of growth the church needs? Perhaps a church *health* movement rather than a church *growth* movement is needed. Maybe we actually undermine the health of our churches by overemphasizing growth.

This is also true for youth groups. While it's possible to make a small youth group grow by using the latest marketing techniques to make the youth program as enticing as possible, the resulting growth will be superficial and temporary at best. Lasting growth, a true indicator that the group is meeting the needs of young people, will more likely come slowly, naturally, and spontaneously as a result of good health.

Proponents of church growth are often quick to remind us that the church does have a responsibility to carry out the Great Commission. Christ's command to "go and make disciples" (Matt. 28:19) is undisputably clear and no more an option for us than it was for the twelve who originally heard Christ utter those words. Yet, Jesus did not prioritize his commands as we sometimes are prone to do. When Jesus was asked which commandments were most important he responded, "Love God and love your neighbor as yourself." But love is a difficult thing to measure, whereas new converts can be counted and added to the rolls of the church. Perhaps our need for quantifiable results keeps us from giving love a greater priority in the church.

There is no question that the mission of the church is to proclaim the Good News to all people. We must be concerned with reaching the world for Christ. But churches and youth groups that are healthy will be in a much better position to fulfill that mission.

A HEALTHY YOUTH GROUP WILL GROW

A primary characteristic of a healthy church and a healthy youth group is community. When Jesus prayed in John 17, he prayed that the church would be *one* "so that the world may believe" (John 17:21). Accordingly, Christian unity will convince the world that the gospel is indeed true. People will find it irresistible. Perhaps what Jesus has prescribed for the church is not so much the adoption of new techniques for church growth as it is a demonstration of unconditional love and unity within the church.

I worked with a small youth group in one church for almost seven years. Our primary emphasis was community-building. As a group, we spent most of our time doing things together to strengthen our sense of community and our relationships with each other. Eventually the group felt much like a family where each member came to know and care deeply for one another.

We never consciously tried to make that little group grow. We did virtually no "outreach" in the evangelistic sense. Yet it grew from a small group of five or six kids to almost thirty during those seven years, a gain of over 500 per cent. The growth happened almost imperceptibly with each new person becoming an important family member. It was good, solid growth.

For example, I'll never forget the first time one of the kids asked, "Um . . . I have a friend who I think would really like our group. . . . Do you think it would be all right if I asked him to come?" I was shocked. For years I had tried to push kids to bring their friends, but to no avail. But now, without any coercion at all, kids were recognizing that there was something special enough about our group to meet the needs of their friends outside the church.

A healthy youth group will grow not only because it is characterized by community, but also because it is a place where committed adults care enough about young people to build relationships with them. Here young people are growing in the faith, involved in ministry, and given real responsibility. And here they laugh and have fun in a positive and safe environment. If your youth group is small and lacks health, growth will not cure it. A larger group will not necessarily become a healthier group. Health must come first.

QUALITY AND CONSISTENCY ARE IMPORTANT

Another way to encourage good growth in a small youth group is to maintain a consistently high standard of quality in your youth ministry. A small youth group does not justify small effort. "All the angels rejoice," Jesus said, over one person who comes into the kingdom of God (Luke 15). The quality of our youth group programs and activities need to reflect the infinite worth of the few who are there.

One of the most common reasons small youth groups fail to grow is that programs, meetings, and activities are conducted in a mediocre fashion because, after all, the group is small. Unless young people have confidence in the group and know that it is consistently worth attending, they will be reluctant to ask anyone else to come. They want to feel proud of their youth group, not embarrassed by it. Furthermore, if and when visitors do come, it is unlikely that they will return if they sense that little care or preparation has gone into the youth program.

For about three years, I played music professionally and had the opportunity to perform in some of the largest arenas and concert halls in America. Perhaps the best advice I ever received during that time was from a record producer who said, "Whenever you perform, no matter how small the crowd is, play like it's Carnegie Hall. Give those people the best you have. You never know who's going to be sitting out there in the audience." The same advice should be heeded by pastors, youth workers, and others who serve the church, only doubly so, because after all, we do know who's sitting out there. It's someone who matters a great deal to Christ and to the church—someone who deserves no less than the best we have to offer.

EMPHASIZE PERSONAL INVITATION

Twenty-five years ago Joseph Bayly wrote a classic called *The Gospel Blimp*. It told the story of a well-meaning Christian man who tried to evangelize his community by utilizing a blimp that circled the town, flashed gospel messages, dumped religious tracts, and broadcast sermonettes from huge loudspeakers. The blimp was a clever caricature of the many outlandish methods we often employ to attract people to Christ. In Bayly's story, the blimp was a colossal failure, but the personal witness of one man who chose to share his faith simply by being a good neighbor was the most successful of all.

The parable of the Gospel Blimp is relevant for us today. Most people are not going to be impressed by elaborate programs and promotional techniques, but they will respond to the personal invitation of a friend. Recent studies have shown that seventy to eighty percent of all people who attend church were invited by someone they knew. Conversely, two-thirds of all nonchurchgoers say they were never invited by anyone. The best way for any youth group to grow intentionally is through personal invitation.

If your youth group is ready to grow and your young people feel truly committed to reaching out to others, it would be worthwhile to discuss with them ways to invite people they already know to youth group. Many young people only need a little encouragement to do so. Often kids are afraid to invite people to church or to youth group because they have never done it before or because they fear rejection or humiliation. For others, the idea of inviting someone to church never crosses their minds.

Here are a few tips to help you help your young people invite others to your youth group:

1. Have the kids make a list of people they know whom they might invite. Some kids never take time to think of specific friends who might be interested in coming.

2. Ask the kids to select one person from that list to invite during the coming week or month. You might want to take time to pray together for that person.

3. Encourage your young people not to give up should they get a negative response the first time around. Most people who do come later jokingly comment, "he kept asking until I finally gave in and came."

4. Remind your young people to have realistic expectations. Not everyone will be able to come. They may need to ask five or ten friends over a long period of time before one person finally says yes. You can help prepare them so that they won't become frustrated and give up too easily.

5. Help your young people not to take rejection personally. Assure them that a "no, thanks" from a friend will not destroy their friendship. In most cases, people consider a personal invitation to participate in something a friend enjoys to be a compliment, not a put-down.

6. Encourage your young people to be specific with their invitations rather than asking someone, "Would you be interested in coming to our youth group sometime?" The invitation should be a specific event on a specific date, at a specific time and place. You might want to provide them with a pass-out flyer giving all the details and a map.

Christian young people need to learn how to invite their friends in a natural sort of way without pressure. Some young people who are outgoing will feel more comfortable than others inviting their friends to church functions. Many kids need "permission" to invite others or a few ideas to get them started. Then, a gentle reminder on occasion will often suffice.

OTHER GOOD WAYS TO ENCOURAGE GROWTH

One of the best ways to introduce new people to your youth group is to invite them to a nonthreatening social activity: a swim party, an evening of games, a trip to an amusement park, a "burger bash," an overnight retreat, or some other special event sponsored by the group. Sometimes young people are reluctant to invite their friends to a church service or a youth group meeting that might seem too "religious" to someone outside the church. But it's not difficult to invite someone to a party.

Encourage young people to bring friends to regular social events. Then make sure that any new young people who do come are welcomed and included in the activities without embarrassing them. Take this opportunity to meet the newcomers and learn a little bit more about them. Let them know they are welcome to attend other youth group functions and be a part of the group if they desire but don't launch a sneak evangelistic attack. Young people will be much more inclined to bring new kids to group activities if they know for certain their friends will not be hit over the head with a gospel message.

You can also take advantage of the U.S. mail to encourage growth. Compile a mailing list that includes all your regular group members, plus prospects. Ask your young people for the names and addresses of friends they would like to include on the youth group mailing list. Then, send out a periodic newsletter or regular announcements. The most effective mailers are those that communicate friendliness, creativity, and a sense of humor. There are dozens of great ideas for letters, flyers, and postcards in the *Ideas* books, published by Youth Specialties.

If none of these strategies for growth bring results, try using mirrors. Cover all four walls of your meeting space with giant mirrors, and presto! . . . Your group will suddenly be huge.

There are many good ways to stimulate growth in a small youth group, but most importantly the best kind of growth comes naturally and usually very slowly. Good growth comes as a result of a healthy youth group, quality and consistency in ministry, and the personal invitation of kids who care about their friends. Our calling as youth workers is not to minister to those who *aren't* in our youth groups, but to those who are. As the master of the servants in one of Jesus' parables said, "You have been faithful with a few things . . . I will put you in charge of many things" (Matt. 25:23).

PART TWO

PROGRAMMING IDEAS FOR SMALL YOUTH GROUPS

6 TEACHING AND LEARNING ACTIVITIES FOR SMALL YOUTH GROUPS

A small youth group provides an ideal setting for effective Christian education and growth. Young people learn better in small groups than they do in large ones. The reasons for this are many. Among them:

1. The youth worker/teacher can give each young person in a small youth group the individual attention they need.

2. In a small class, the youth worker/teacher can modify the curriculum and be innovative as well as creative.

3. In a small group, students get to know each other better, as well as their leaders. This promotes constructive growth by comparing and contrasting ideas.

4. The kids in a small youth group develop a greater sense of self-worth when they see that the youth worker/teacher takes time for them and their needs.

5. Small group meetings tend to be more activity-oriented than lecture-oriented, promoting experiential learning and discovery.

6. Young people in a small group are more likely to have the opportunity to express their opinions, ask questions, and get the feedback they need to help make decisions and draw conclusions.

7. In a small youth group, each person's presence and participation matters, greatly increasing motivation and responsibility for learning.

THE ACTIVITY ADVANTAGE

One important educational advantage of a small youth group is that it is much more conducive to activity or student-centered learning than lecture or teacher-centered learning. In a large group, the lecture method is usually the best way to communicate information quickly, but it has definite limitations. Most educators agree that listening to a lecture is at the very bottom of the list of "effective learning strategies." It has been said that the lecture method is "the quickest way to get information from the teacher's mouth to the student's notebook without having it pass through the student's mind."

Fortunately, lectures don't work well with a small youth group. As any public speaker will testify, it is very difficult to give an inspiring or motivating talk to a small group of four for five people. On the other hand, it's not difficult to lead a small group in an activity or exercise that gets them involved. The potential for learning increases dramatically when the learners are involved in the learning process. Small youth groups are great places to learn because the emphasis is on student participation rather than teacher pontification.

Here is a partial list of learning activities you can do with a small youth group:

Have a discussion.
Do a role play.
Play a simulation game.
Go on a field trip.
Do creative writing.
Brainstorm ideas.
Make a film, video, or slide show.
Do a values clarification exercise.
Compose a song or rewrite hymns.
Make banners and posters.
Publish a newspaper.
Have a debate.
Perform a drama.
Take a quiz.
Interview a guest.
Read together, aloud or silently.
Do research.
Visit another church.
Critique a movie.
Critique the sermon.
Listen to a record.
Solve a problem.
Sing in a choir.
Have a retreat.
Do some artwork.
Do a service project.
Serve on a committee.
Paint a mural.
Have a Bible study.

THE IMPORTANCE OF DISCUSSION

One of the primary reasons a small youth group is a great place to learn is because a small youth group is a great place to have a discussion. With a large youth group, the emphasis must be on planning and presenting interesting and entertaining programs; with a small youth group, the emphasis is on creating an atmosphere for discussion. Whether it is two or twenty people discussing a topic, the interaction produced by a good, lively discussion greatly increases the potential for learning. Here are ten reasons why:

1. Discussion gets each young person involved. Learners are learning because they are involved. You can't be a mere spectator in a good discussion.

2. Discussion puts the subject in the student's own language. Kids will have a better understanding of the topic when they can verbalize it themselves.

3. Discussion lifts truth out of a vacuum and puts it into the real world. A discussion allows young people to take what they are hearing and put it on trial as they discuss it in the context of the world where they live. A simple statement like "God is love," for example, can be carefully examined, tested, questioned, and explored from a variety of vantage points. If it really is true, it will survive such scrutiny.

4. Discussion increases the interest level of the group due to the variety of viewpoints expressed, the controversy that is often generated, and the opportunity given to participate. And because the interest level increases, retention also increases.

5. Discussion helps to improve communication skills. Everyone needs to learn the "three R's—readin', 'ritin', and relatin'." Young people need to learn how to communicate in good basic English, both orally and in writing, and they also need to learn how to relate to other people. All of life involves communication. One of the greatest gifts we can give our young people is the opportunity to express themselves and their ideas in clear propositional statements to each other.

6. Discussion encourages young people to think and to question, rather than accepting everything at face value. News commentator Dan Rather once said, "In modern society, perhaps the most understimulated organ in the human body is the brain," and he may be correct. We need to teach our young people how to think.

7. Questions do not go unasked. They may be unanswered, but at least they aren't ignored. A discussion allows young people to express their feelings, their doubts, and their questions and to receive feedback from others.

8. Discussion enhances a young person's creativity. Active discussion involves a search for truth and alternatives to problems, thus exercising the creative abilities of young people.

9. Discussion builds community in a youth group. When people talk to each other, the possibility of their drawing closer together and better understanding each other increases.

10. Discussion allows the leader to learn more about the young people in the group. As kids express their ideas and opinions, you gain valuable insight into their level of maturity and commitment, thus enabling you to minister to them more effectively.

LEADING A DISCUSSION

A good discussion doesn't just "happen"; but it requires preparation and leadership. It is not something you do when you forget to prepare your lesson or when you need a "filler." A poorly prepared discussion can be frustrating, boring, and often intimidating to young people, producing a negative result.

A good discussion is not a debate or an argument. Neither is it a pooling of ignorance. It is not a contest to see who can sound the most intelligent or say the most outrageous things. There are no winners or losers in a discussion. You aren't trying to get kids to say all the right things or to come up with all the right answers. Instead, a discussion is a "shared pursuit of truth through cooperation among all the group members." It has direction and purpose and goes somewhere. The leader guides the discussion intentionally, keeping it on course and helping it to arrive at its destination. A good discussion will generally follow these steps:

1. The "significant event" or the presentation. This is sometimes called the "discussion starter." It can be a film, a role play, a simulation game, a magazine article, a drama, a sermon, or a record. In most cases, the better the discussion starter, the better the discussion.

2. Understanding the meaning of the "significant event." This is when you deal with questions like "What was the film trying to say?"; "What conclusions did the author of the article make?"; "What did you see or hear?"

3. Group response. Here you get the group's positive and negative intellectual and emotional reactions to the "significant event" or the problem as it has been stated. "Do you agree or disagree?"

4. Bring in new information. At this point, you might want to introduce additional information or another resource that perhaps presents a supporting or contradictory viewpoint. For example, you might read some scripture passages that deal with the topic or the problem under discussion.

5. Considering implications and consequences. If possible, the group can attempt to arrive at a consensus or draw some conclusions based upon the ideas presented and the viewpoints expressed. Perhaps the group could brainstorm some solutions or possible alternatives that are available.

6. Decision-making. The final phase of the discussion is deciding what the implications are for us. What difference does it make in our lives? Kids can be given the opportunity to think through these questions and to decide what they must do with what they have learned. One good way to facilitate this part of the discussion is to have the kids complete the sentence "I learned . . ." or "What I want to remember from this discussion is . . ."

Of course, no discussion will be as simple, as orderly, or as well-defined as these six steps might indicate. Nor should it be. Young people will often have their own ideas about where a discussion should go, and sometimes it is best to "go with the flow." Never force kids to conform to any preconceived agenda during a discussion. The important thing to understand is that a discussion is not chaotic but has direction and purpose—a beginning, a middle, and an end. There will always be a fair amount of "unknowns" and risks in a discussion. But an effective leader will know how to keep things under control, enable young people to discover new ideas, and learn from the experience.

The art of leading a discussion is best learned from experience; however, there are a number of "dos and don'ts" that can help you to achieve greater success.

1. Set up your meeting room properly for a discussion. Make sure the room is conducive to a conversational atmosphere. The seating arrangement should be casual, either in a circular or random configuration. It is best for the leader to be seated with the group. This communicates to the kids that you are a co-learner, participant, and facilitator, rather than an "expert."

2. Prepare a few key questions ahead of time but don't limit yourself to them. Add "flow questions" during the discussion to keep things moving and to probe deeper into issues that are raised. This means, of course, that you will need to be a listener. Keep a pencil and paper handy and make notes during the discussion when someone says something that needs to be explored further or when you think of another good question that needs to be discussed.

3. Ask "open ended" questions that allow kids to express their opinions and "best guesses." For example, rather than asking, "What is the meaning of this phrase?" ask instead, "What *do you think* the meaning of this phrase is?"

4. Begin with nonthreatening questions and then move to deeper, more thought-provoking ones. If necessary, start with some light "just for fun" questions such as "If you won the New York state lottery, what is the first thing you would buy with the money?" You might even want to share an answer of your own to get the discussion started. Another good opening question is a "complete the sentence" question like "The most important thing in my life right now is . . ." Have the kids share a one or two word response.

5. Use appropriate discussion techniques for your group. For example, if your group has few "talkers," you might want to begin by having kids write out their responses to a question anonymously on a slip of paper. When completed, you can read them to the group.

Another technique is the "circular response" in which you go around the circle and allow each person to share his or her response to the question. If you do this, make sure that the question is one that everyone can answer and allow kids to "pass" if they don't want to share.

Another possibility is to breakdown the group into diads (twos) or triads (threes) to discuss a particular question. After a designated time, they can reunite and share the results of their discussions with the entire group.

6. Don't force kids to talk. Instead, try to create an atmosphere in which they feel comfortable enough to volunteer.

7. Stay on the topic. An occasional "tangent" might be worth pursuing, but it is generally best to refocus the discussion on the primary question or issue whenever it strays too far.

8. The leader should remain as neutral as possible in the discussion. Don't put anyone down for a "wrong" answer or one you don't agree with. Similarly, don't overly congratulate those who give "correct" answers. Then kids will give you responses that they think you want to hear. Instead, affirm everyone, encourage honesty and openness, save your comments for last.

9. Sometimes it's helpful to establish a few "ground rules" for discussion: "Only one person talks at a time."; "If someone says something you don't agree with, don't interrupt or punch him in the nose. Wait until *after* the meeting and *then* punch him in the nose. (Just kidding.)"

10. Don't be afraid to leave a discussion unfinished or a problem unresolved. Sometimes it's very beneficial for kids to go home with more questions than answers. It gives them something to think about for the rest of the week. They may even continue the discussion at home with their parents or with friends. Pick up the discussion, perhaps with some new input, the following week.

11. Wrap up the discussion by summarizing what has been said or by sharing some of your own thoughts on the subject. Your comments should not appear to be the "last word" on the subject but should help them formulate their own responses and to make their own decisions on the issue.

Good discussion is always appropriate for a small youth group. Every activity, film, lecture, field trip, or study should include an opportunity for discussion and discovery. You'll find that the more your kids discuss issues together, the more they will find it to be easy and natural. There are hundreds of excellent ideas for discussion and discussion starters everywhere, from your morning newspaper to the Youth Specialties *Ideas* books.

IDEAS FOR LEARNING, COMMUNITY-BUILDING, AND SPIRITUAL GROWTH

A small youth group also provides an optimal setting for activity-centered learning as well as discussion-centered learning. We must seize every opportunity to make smallness work to the advantage of our young people and ourselves.

There are, of course, literally hundreds of different places to go for good educational materials and learning strategies. Most of them are usable with small youth groups. Remember that no curriculum or lesson is perfect for your group. You will need to choose carefully what to use and adapt the material to fit the needs of your kids.

Here is a selection of outstanding discussion starters and learning activities that have appeared in the Youth Specialities *Ideas* books. Most of these ideas are of a "general" rather than specific nature. This allows greater flexibility in their usage and application.

A-TEAM

A-Team actually stands for "Answer Team." This is a problem-solving exercise that stimulates discussion. Before you begin, write a number of problems or questions like those below on slips of paper and place them in a bowl. Then, have the kids divide into A-Teams, which should be no larger than three or four.

Have each team draw a question from the bowl and go somewhere to work on a solution or an answer. Allow approximately ten minutes. When the teams return, have each team read their question and the solution. The rest of the group can decide whether they agree with the answer. If there is disagreement, the group can discuss the issue together.

The questions below are only suggestions. Most of the time, young people are able to come up with some very thoughtful responses to difficult questions such as these when they are given the opportunity.

1. I don't get it. If Christianity is true, why are there so many religions that call themselves Christian? I mean, what's the difference between Baptists, Presbyterians, etc.?

2. If you ask me, the Christian religion makes you a "doormat," always loving and turning the other cheek stuff.

3. What if I lived like hell for eighty years and then became a Christian on my death bed? Would Billy Graham and I go to the same place?

4. I've been reading through the Old Testament and I'm puzzled. Why did God order his people to kill everybody—even women and children—when they conquered a land? What kind of God is that?

5. Your mother and I do not believe in all this Jesus stuff and we think you spend too much time in church. So we want you to stay away from church for awhile.

6. If God is a god, then why can't we see Him or it? Why don't you prove that God exists? Go ahead . . . prove it to me.

7. The Bible has some nice little stories in it, but everyone knows it's full of contradictions, errors, and myths. How can you believe it?

8. I know a bunch of people that go to your church and they're supposed to be Christians, but I also know what they do during the week and at parties that I attend. They're phonies. If Christianity is so great, why are there so many phonies?

9. My little brother died of leukemia, and I prayed like crazy. Don't tell me there's a God who loves us. Why didn't He help my brother?

10. Look, I know I'm overweight and even though it hurts me to say it, I'm ugly. I started coming to your church because I thought the kids in your youth group would treat me differently than the kids do at school. Wrong! They ignore me and make fun of me just like everyone else. Why?

11. I'm not very attractive. People avoid me and I can tell that most of the people I know make fun of me behind my back. Frankly, I'm ugly. I know it and so does everyone else. What can I do?

12. My parents make me go to church. I like the youth program, but the worship service is a drag. Our minister is irrelevant and boring, and the services don't relate to me at all.

13. My mother is dying of cancer. Every day I'm faced with cancer's ugly and depressing toll on my mom. I am forced to accept more and more of her responsibilities at home. But I like to go out with my friends, too. I feel guilty when I go somewhere and have a good time, but if I stay home, I get angry and frustrated. What's the answer?

14. I've always been told that kids who smoke grass and drink really don't enjoy it. I haven't done any of those things partly because I believed that and partly because I didn't think it was a Christian thing to do, at least until a few weeks ago. I tried pot and drinking, and it was great. I never had so much fun in my life. How can something so good be bad? Did the people who told me these things were bad lie?

AD VALUES

Give each person in the group a selection of magazines with plenty of advertisements in them. Then give each person a list of values like the ones below. Have the kids look through the magazines and match the ads with the values on their list. When they see an ad that appeals to a certain value, then they make a mark beside that value. Here is a sample list:

Wealth, luxury, greed
Security (no worries)
Sexual or physical attractiveness
Intelligence
Conformity (join the crowd)
Freedom (do what you want—no responsibility)
Justice, human rights (concern for others)
Power, strength
Responsibility
Ego, pride
Status (being looked up to)
Escapism
Humility, self-sacrifice

Self-control

Ease, comfort

After everyone has finished, discuss the results. What conclusions can you find about the kind of values that most advertisements present or appeal to? Do they bring out the best or the worst in people? Do very many ads appeal to "Christian" values? This exercise can sensitize young people to be more aware of the ads they see.

AMERICAN BANDSTAND

For an effective program about rock music, have an "American Bandstand" night. Bring in a selection of popular rock records and have the kids vote for the ones they like best, according to certain criteria. You might find it worthwhile to copy the lyrics so that your kids will be able to follow along while listening. Before the kids rate the songs, discuss each of the three criteria so that they know what each one means. Play the records and have the kids judge them using the following criteria:

1. Lyrics: What is the message of the song? Does it support or contradict Christian values and the Word of God?

2. The Artist: What is he or she like as a person? Is the artist a good role model for Christian young people, avoiding behavior that offends followers of Christ?

3. Overall Effect of the Song: Does this song make you feel more positive about your faith or about life? Or more negative? Does it strengthen you as a Christian or weaken you? Or is it neutral?

You may want to add another category: *The Music.* In this category, kids decide whether the record would be considered "good music."

After the kids have rated all the songs, take your results and come up with your own youth group's "Top 10" or "Top 5." This activity can help kids have a better sensitivity to what they hear.

AWARENESS OF OTHERS

Have one person in the group go out of the room for a short time (pick someone who doesn't embarrass very easily). Ask the rest of the group to describe what the person was wearing. Be as specific as possible. Then bring the person back in and let everyone see what he was wearing. Begin your session on awareness this way. Most groups will remember very little specifically about the clothing. From this realization, you can talk about the shallowness of our everyday contacts with people. Discuss our ability as Christians to perceive other's needs and minister to needs. Point out that noticing things about others is something that must be practiced. Recall Christ's perception of needs, how He relied on God the Father for help in this area, and what this means to our ability of perception.

DEAR ABBY

This activity is a simple yet effective way to give kids the opportunity to minister to each other and to provide you with insight into the concerns and problems of individuals in your group.

Each person is given a piece of paper and pencil. The kids are then instructed to write a "Dear Abby" letter. They should think of an unresolved problem and explain it in letter form to a newspaper columnist like Abby or Ann Landers. The letter can be signed "Confused," "Frustrated," or with any name other than the real one.

After everyone has finished, collect the papers and redistribute them so that everyone has someone else's letter. Each person now becomes Abby or Ann Landers and writes a helpful answer. Allow plenty of time. When the answers are completed, collect the papers once again.

Now read the letters to the group one at a time, along with the answers. Discuss them, asking the group whether the advice given was good or bad. Other solutions to the problem can be suggested by the group. Kids may be able to give sincere, sensible, and practical help to each other.

THE GOSSIP GAME

The Scriptures have a great deal to say about the consequences of idle gossip or "murdering with the tongue." The following game demonstrates the seriousness of spreading rumors.

Choose three young people to leave the room while a fourth person copies (as best as he can) onto poster board a picture that he is shown.

One of the three persons outside comes in and draws the same drawing, using the first person's drawing as the guide, rather than the original.

The next person comes in and draws his drawing from the second person's, and likewise with the last person.

The last person's drawing is then compared with the original, and of course, there will be hardly any resemblance to the original. Each one draws another's copy, and everyone changes the drawing a little, usually omitting or adding what he considers important. This game is entertaining as well as revealing and can be followed with a discussion about gossip and communication.

HOW MANY F'S?

Here is a fun little experiment about awareness. Print up some sheets like the one below and give one to each person in the group face down. Everyone turns the page over and begins at the same time. Each person should work alone.

Read the following sentence in the enclosed block. After reading the sentence, go back and count the F's. You have *one* minute.

```
FINISHED FILES ARE THE RE-
SULT OF YEARS OF SCIENTIF-
IC STUDY COMBINED WITH
THE EXPERIENCE OF YEARS.
```

Number of F's in the block _____

Try it yourself before you read the answer below.

Most people will count three. Others will see four or five. Only a few will count all six F's that are in the box. After the sixty seconds are up, ask the group how many F's they counted, and you will get a variety of answers. Those who counted only three, four, or five will be quite surprised when you tell them the answer. But after they find all six F's, they will feel rather silly that they didn't see them in the first place. Most people tend to overlook the word "OF" when they are counting because they are looking only at the bigger words.

This test is often given to people in driving classes to demonstrate how we often fail to see motorcycles on the road because they are so small, and because we aren't looking for them. This lesson can also be applied to people. We often miss the good qualities in other people because we aren't looking for them. We tend to look instead for bad qualities that we want to see, making ourselves look good by comparison.

Follow up with an exercise like "What Others Think of Me" (see page 77) in which kids look for the good qualities in each other and affirm each other's gifts and abilities. When good qualities are emphasized, they become more obvious and raise everyone's self-esteem.

MADISON AVENUE

For a youth meeting where you want to combine fun with learning, get a video camera or a super-8 camera with sound that can photograph indoors. Divide your group into teams, making certain that everyone is involved and have them develop a sixty-second commercial to sell Christianity to the world. The most fun is for them to do a "take-off" on a well-known TV commercial, adapting it to Christianity. Within a week or two view the commercials. All the kids will love to see themselves on film. Then discuss the feasibility of presenting an accurate picture of Christianity in sixty seconds.

A PENNY FOR YOUR THOUGHTS

Here's a crazy but effective way to get kids into discussions.

Ask each of the kids to bring twenty pennies and a nickel for the next discussion (topical or general sharing of ideas). The kids sit in a circle around a plastic pot made from a baby's potty chair. The leader poses a question and each person in the circle tosses in a "penny for his thoughts" on the subject. If someone wants to interject a statement (more than just a sentence), it is called "putting in your two cents worth," and the person must put in two cents. If a person cannot think of anything to say when it's his turn, he may "four-feit" only once and does so by throwing in a nickel and getting back a penny.

When the discussion is over, the money collected can go to a worthy cause or be awarded to the kid who talked too much.

PARAPHRASING THE LOVE CHAPTER

Here is a way to allow kids the opportunity to put some of their own thoughts into the Love Chapter of the Bible, I Corinthians 13. By doing an exercise such as this with any portion of Scripture, kids are forced to think through the meaning and application of the passage. Omit key words or phrases but keep the basic idea. Ask the kids to fill in the blanks with whatever they think fits best. Afterwards, compare with the original message. Here is an example. Print it up and pass it out. Let each person read his completed version to the entire group.

I Corinthians 13

If I have all the ability to talk about _____, but have no love, then I am nothing but a big mouth. If I had all the power to _____, but
have no love, then my life is a waste of time. If I understand everything
about _____, but have no love, then I might as well sit in a gutter. If I
give away everything that I have, but have no love, then I _____.
Love is patient, love is kind, love is _____. Love never _____.

THE POOR MAN'S HOLY LAND TOUR

This idea is great for a small youth group because of the group's mobility. Announce that you are going to take the group on a tour of the Holy Land, and then escort them to places within walking or driving distance that resemble biblical locations. For example, take them to the tallest building in town and lead a Bible study there about Satan tempting Jesus to jump from the high mountain. The options are endless: Jewish synagogue, a mountainside for the Sermon on the Mount, a garden for the Garden of Gethsemane, an upstairs room for the Last Supper, and old boiler room for the story of the Hebrew children in the fiery furnace, a country road for the story of Paul's Damascus road experience, and a lakefront for a wilderness area. Using nature as a visual aid is worth a thousand flannelgraphs.

This tour doesn't have to be done all in one day. Remember one of the advantages of a small youth group is that you are not limited to meet in one particular place. Anytime you are preparing a lesson from Scripture, you might consider taking the group to some location that would enhance the study.

For example, if you are studying one of Paul's letters from prison, you might want to see if you could arrange to have your group locked in a jail cell for the study or perhaps arrange a guided tour of a jail, prison, or detention facility. It's a very sobering experience for most kids, and the scripture passages suddenly become much more meaningful. A field trip such as this can be a valuable learning experience.

PROGRESSIVE WORSHIP SERVICE

Here's an interesting way to involve young people in worship. It can be done in a church, in homes, or on a weekend retreat. There's no limit to its possibilities. It works just like a progressive dinner.

A worship service has a variety of elements, just like a dinner does. By participating in each element of worship separately and in a different location, it provides a good opportunity to teach young people what a worship is. Acts 2:42 and Colossians 3:16 provide a good scriptural base. Here's one way to do it:

1. Fellowship: Begin with some kind of group interaction or sharing that provides a chance for the kids to get to know one another better. Create a celebrative, but not rowdy mood.

2. Spiritual Songs: At the next location, have someone lead the group in a variety of well-known hymns and favorite songs of worship.

3. Prayer Move to another location that provides a good atmosphere for prayer. If outside, a garden would be nice, as Jesus often chose a garden for prayer. Have the kids offer prayer requests and thanksgivings and lead in prayer.

4. Scripture Reading: At the next location, have several kids read a lesson from the Old Testament, the New Testament, and perhaps the Psalms. Use a modern English translation.

5. Teaching: The next stop can be where the sermon is preached. If you prefer, you could accomplish the same results without being "preachy" by substituting a dialogue sermon or a film.

6. Breaking of Bread (Communion): The last place can be around the Lord's table, with a communion service. Conduct this however you choose, but it should be a time of celebration and joy.

There are other ingredients such as the offering that you can incorporate into these or take separately. Design your own progressive worship service, and your group will never forget it.

QUESTION BOX

To evaluate whether you are meeting the needs of your kids, try this. Construct a box with a slit in the top to collect questions that the kids would like to have answered. Place the box in a conspicuous place and allow kids to drop their questions on any subject into the box each week. Allow time each week during every meeting to answer questions that were submitted the week before. The group could respond to questions in discussion format.

A question box can also be used to prepare for the following week's program. If, for example, you are planning a program about love and dating, tell the kids to write out a question on that subject and drop it in the box. This is a great way to keep your finger on the pulse of your youth group.

ROLE-PLAYS

Role-playing can be used very effectively with a small youth group to stimulate discussion and learning. Youth workers sometimes fear that role-play requires "good acting," or participants who are extroverts. However, anyone can take part in role-play and enjoy the experience as well as learn from it.

Essentially, role-play is nothing more than pretending to be someone else. Little children role-play all the time. Unfortunately, adults "grow out of such nonsense." Good role-plays for Christian education usually include assuming someone else's point of view. Here is an example of a popular role-play from the Bible:

Person #1:   You are Joseph, of Bethlehem, and you are engaged to a young girl whose name is Mary.

Person #2:   You are Mary, and you are engaged to Joseph, but you have just discovered that you are pregnant with the Christ child.

Situation: Mary, you must explain your pregnancy to Joseph, who is unaware of it or its circumstances. Joseph, you should react as any normal person would in your situation.

In this role-play, the two characters simply "become" Mary and Joseph. They talk to each other based upon their understanding and knowledge of the situation and how they think the actual characters might have responded. Of course, the Bible does not tell us what actually took place, which is why this makes a good role-play. There is no "right" or "wrong" way to do it.

You can role-play other biblical situations, or you can role-play modern ones. Here is another example:

Person #1:   You are a fifteen-year-old boy and like rock music. This weekend your favorite rock group is in town for a big concert. All your friends are going.

Person #2:   You are #1's father. You have done some checking and discovered that the rock concert this weekend will more than likely feature sex and violence on stage and booze and drugs in the audience. You have decided that your son will not go.

Situation: Person #1—You should try to convince your father that you should be allowed to attend the rock concert. Person #2—You should remain firm in your position that the rock concert is off limits.

With a small youth group, the best way to do role-play is to have the two role-players do the role-play in the center of the room in two chairs while the rest of the group looks on. If the group is new to role-playing, have your adult leaders do a sample role-play first, then ask a couple of volunteers to give it a try.

After the role-play, lead a discussion with the entire group based on what they saw happen in the role-play. Questions could include "What were the strong and weak points made by each person?" or "If you had been person #1 or person #2, what would you have said?" Such a discussion will start the kids talking about the topic under consideration.

Role-plays, like discussion itself, becomes easier and less threatening the more you do them. They work well with a small youth group because everyone can participate and the size of the audience is less intimidating to the role-players.

An excellent role-playing resource for small youth groups is *Roll-a-Role*, available from Youth Specialties (1224 Greenfield Dr., El Cajon, CA 92021). It contains over one hundred topics, and the roles are determined simply by rolling two foam rubber cubes. Instructions are included in the game kit. Write Youth Specialties for ordering information.

SHARE AN ADULT

Invite adults in your church or from the community to visit your youth group to share their occupations. You might ask them to tell how they got started in their particular career and whether they think young people should enter the same profession. They might also share how their business or occupation is affected by their being a Christian. Allow the young people to ask questions about such issues as ethics, goals, and job security.

SHOPPING SPREE

For a creative look at money and how people spend it, here is a simple simulation to try with your young people. Buy or print several million dollars in play money. Then, divide it into random amounts ($3,000 to $450,000) placed in plain envelopes. Pass out these envelopes to your group.

Set up a table or bulletin board with a wide assortment of full-page advertisements for cars, mansions, computers, vacations, food, savings accounts, and Christian relief efforts. Each youth gets an order blank to "buy" any items he wishes, as long as they can pay for it themselves or by pooling their money. Give them ten minutes to "shop" and five minutes to fill in their order blanks.

Gather all of the order blanks or compile a blackboard list of everything ordered. Discuss the values expressed, their feelings about unequal distribution of the cash, and their responsibility to care for the needy.

SHARING CUBES

Make a pair of large "dice" out of foam rubber or cardboard. On the six sides of each cube, write instructions for sharing. Here are some sample ones:

Describe your week.

Share a frustration.

Share a prayer request.

Compliment someone.

One at a time, each person chooses one of the cubes and "rolls it" on the floor. He or she then shares briefly, according to the instruction that turns up. If you have more than eight to ten people in your group, break into smaller groups and give each group one of the cubes.

TALK IT OVER

This game is great for giving your people a fun, nonthreatening way to communicate what they believe to each other. It will also help them get to know each other better.

To play you will need one deck of playing cards for every two people and a list of phrases like the ones below that express an opinion or belief:

1. I would leave a party shortly after arriving if I weren't having a good time.

2. I would discuss my personal family problems with friends.

3. There are some crimes for which the death penalty should apply.

4. If I were offered a less satisfying job at 25% increase in salary, I would take it.

5. Parents should stay home from a long-awaited party to attend a sick child.

6. I could forgive and forget if my mate were unfaithful.

7. I think laundry is woman's work.

8. I think any teenager who wants birth control pills should be allowed to get them with no hassle.

9. I would ask a friend to stop smoking around me if the smoke bothered me.

10. A parent should immediately defend a child if the other parent were punishing him unfairly.

11. There should be no secrets between good friends.

12. Housework done by the female is usually taken for granted by the male.

13. I think there should be sex education in schools starting in kindergarten.

14. I think there should be sex education in churches.

15. Children should be spanked for some types of misbehavior.

16. If a man enjoys housework and a woman enjoys a career, they should pursue these roles.

17. It's the duty of parents to attend school functions in which their child is participating.

18. I think it is important to remember birthdays of family and friends.

19. I think it's okay for a thirteen year old to see an R rated movie.

20. Women with small children should not work unless it's a financial necessity.

21. Marijuana should be legalized.

22. Kids shouldn't have to account for their allowance.

23. Parents should regulate how much television a small child can watch.

24. Schools should eliminate the use of grades.

25. I would say something if I saw a friend littering.

You can, of course, make up your own statements. Duplicate enough copies of the list so that each person has one.

Have the kids pair off to play the game. It's best to put kids together who aren't best friends. They should sit across from each other, on the floor or at tables, face-to-face. Each player should have half of a deck of cards (two suits).

The suits should be separated so that each player has two stacks of cards, each of the same suit. The only cards used in the game are the Ace and the numbered cards, two through ten. The players should also have a list of the statements.

One of the players begins the game by reading a statement from the list. Both players then secretly choose a card from one set of the cards between one (Ace) and ten: "one" indicates total *disagreement* and ten indicates total *agreement* with the statement. The other cards represent various shades of agreement or disagreement. The chosen card is then placed face down to each player's *left*.

Next, each player tries to guess the other player's position by choosing a card from the other set of cards and placing it face down to his *right* (which would be next to the other player's first card). In other words, the "me" cards are placed down on the left, and the "you" cards are placed on the right. Now there are four cards face down. At this point, the players turn over the cards.

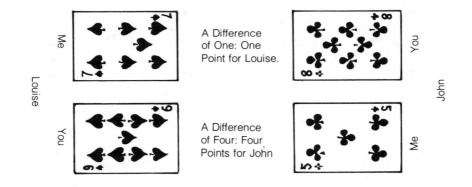

A Difference of One: One Point for Louise.

A Difference of Four: Four Points for John

Players score points by noting the difference between the value of their right hand card (the "you" card) and their partner's "me" card. For example, let's say John and Louise are playing this game. John places a nine to his right, thinking that Louise strongly agrees with the statement. Louise, however, has rated her own position with a five. John's score is four. Meanwhile, Louise has placed an eight on her right to indicate what, in her estimation, is John's position on the statement. John has rated himself with a seven. So, the score for Louise is one.

As the game progresses, the object is to keep your score as low as possible. The "winner" of the game is the one with the lowest score at the end of the time limit.

If on any statement the difference between the two players' "me" cards is more than four, then they should "talk it over" for two or three minutes before moving on to the next statement. This allows kids to discuss their differences with each other and to try to defend their points of view.

Here is a much simpler version of this game: Players get into small groups of any size, up to five in a group. Each player has one set of cards, numbered one through ten. A statement is read, and each player simply picks one card indicating his position on the issue. All at the same time, they reveal their cards to each other, and if there is a difference of more than two between any two players in the group, the group needs to "talk it over." There is no "scoring" in this version of the game.

TENSION GETTERS

A "Tension Getter" is a short story about people who are caught in a crossfire of values. In most cases, a Tension Getter sets up a decision or choice that must be made, and the choice is rarely an easy one. As the name implies, Tension Getters intentionally create tension, forcing young people to apply their values and their faith to difficult dilemmas, not unsimilar to those they will face.

Tension Getters make excellent discussion starters for small youth groups. There are two Tension Getters books now available, *Tension Getters* and *Tension Getters II*, (Zondervan).

Here's an example:

Take A Hard Look

Mary and Bill, two friends of yours, have decided to get an apartment together as soon as they graduate from school. They believe it is better for them to live together instead of getting married right away. Both of their parents are divorced, and they don't want the same thing to happen to their relationship. Mary and Bill believe that living together will be a good way to test their relationship. If things work out, they plan to marry in a few years. Bill and Mary value your opinion and want to know what you think.

What would you do?

Reason:

What should you do?

Reason:

THANKSGIVING EXCHANGE

This is a good discussion starter for Thanksgiving or for any time when you want to teach a lesson about gratitude. It works best with a group that knows each other fairly well. Begin by having each person share one or two things for which he is thankful, usually that which is most obvious to him.

Then have each person write his name on the top of a sheet of paper. Collect the sheets and redistribute them so that everyone has a sheet with someone else's name on it. Now have each person write on that sheet what he would be thankful for if he were the person whose name is on that sheet. He can list as many things as he wants.

Following this, pass the sheets back to the person whose name is on each sheet and discuss the following questions:

1. What things are written on your sheet that you haven't thanked God for lately?

2. What things are written on your sheet that you hadn't ever thought about thanking God for?

3. Is anything written on your sheet that you disagree with or that you don't think you should be thankful for?

This exercise helps young people realize that they often take for granted many things for which they should be thankful.

THEATER THEOLOGY

Young people are attending movies now more than ever before. So it is a good idea to use certain films that are current at the local cinema as teaching tools rather than to avoid them. Many theaters will give group rates for Saturday matinees. Plan to attend a film with your entire youth group. After the film, have an informal time of discussion, allowing kids to share their impressions of the movie's content. Prepare questions such as these ahead of time:

1. What was the main theme of the film?

2. Did you identify with one of the characters in the film more than others?

3. Were any "answers" provided in the movie?

4. How would you have ended the movie or how would you have liked for the movie to end?

5. Can you learn any lessons from this movie?

It's important for you as leader to preview the movie ahead of time, and if you are in a more "conservative" church, to clear this activity with parents and church leadership. You may find that the secular cinema is much better for communicating truth than traditional gospel flicks.

THEOLOGICAL FICTIONARY

If your young people sometimes get stumped trying to figure out the meanings of those big "theological" words, here's a game that will whittle those words down to size. It's played like the game "Dictionary," found on page 85.

Make a list of words like "justification," "atonement," "sanctification," and "vicarious," then read them to the group. Taking the words one at a time, have each person come up with a definition for that word. The correct definition is not given by the leader until after everyone has given their definition. If a person is not sure, he should make up a definition that sounds good.

Scoring is as follows:

1. For getting the correct definition—five points.

2. For each time someone agrees with your "phony" definition—five points.

As the game progresses, it would be wise to "rotate" so that each person has a chance to be the first guesser, improving their chances that someone will go along with their definition. You might want to allow kids to change their answer after all the definitions have been given, but before the "official" correct definition has been given. The person with the most points is the winner of the game. You'll be surprised at the ingenuity of your kids to come up with wild new theological definitions.

UNITY

This exercise helps the group to understand the concept of unity. Begin by reading the first sixteen verses of Ephesians 4. Discuss with the group what they think unity means for us today.

Then, pass out enough "Tinker Toys" so that every member of the group has plenty to work with. Ask each person to take their Tinker Toys somewhere where he can work alone to construct something that represents himself. After the group has done this, have everyone return and describe his creation to the rest of the group, explaining some of its symbolism.

Next, have the kids pair off, and instruct each pair to try to connect their two Tinker Toy creations into one. They might want to symbolically join their objects at particular places to communicate special meanings. After each pair has joined objects, have the pairs get together with other pairs, and continue to join all the objects together until finally they are all one big creation. Further discussion may develop. You might want to keep the big Tinker Toy object on display for a period of time as a reminder to the group of the unity they have in Christ.

WHAT OTHERS THINK OF ME

This is a community-building exercise that allows kids to affirm each other and to provide each other with some constructive advice.

Give each person a slip of paper, approximately 3 x 8 inches. Have him write his name at the bottom and a one-word self-description at the top. Each one is then instructed to fold the paper down from the top twice to conceal the word he wrote. The paper should look like this:

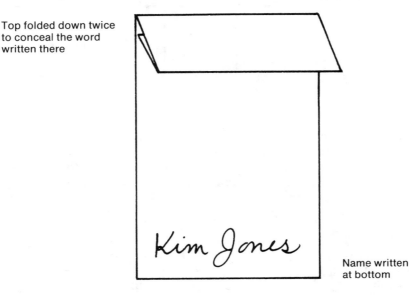

Top folded down twice to conceal the word written there

Kim Jones

Name written at bottom

Kids are to exchange papers twice, so that no one knows for sure who has whose paper. Each person then writes at the top of the page a one-word description of the person named at the bottom. Kids should be instructed to be honest, constructive, and as helpful as possible to the person they are describing. If they don't know the person, they should leave it blank. The papers are folded down to conceal the word they wrote, and then exchanged again and the process is repeated until the papers are full of one-word descriptions of the person named at the bottom.

The completed papers are returned back to the person whose name is at the bottom, and the kids are given a few minutes to look them over. Each person can then compare their own self-image with how others think of them. Discussion can follow, with young people sharing their feelings about the exercise and what their response to it will be.

WHERE DO YOU STAND?

This is learning strategy that you can use with almost any topic. Make five colored squares out of cardboard, large enough for several kids to stand on. The colors of the six squares, and their positions on the floor should look like this:

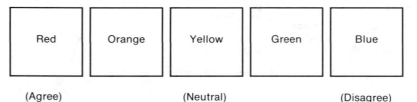

Next, think up a number of hypothetical situations that involve making value choices, such as "A baby is born with a serious birth defect that would make the child unable to live without constant care in an institution. Should the child be allowed to die?" Or, another example: "A woman is a prisoner in a concentration camp. Her husband and children are waiting for her in a nearby neutral country. The only possible way she can be freed from this prison is to become pregnant because pregnant women are automatically released. Would it be right for her to have sexual relations with another man so that she can become pregnant?"

The young people are to decide what they think, then stand on one of the colored squares. The blue square represents total disagreement, and the red square represents total agreement. The other shades are in-between. If someone felt undecided, but leaned a little toward the "wrong" side, then he might stand on the green square. After everyone has chosen a place to stand, ask each one to share why he feels this way. During the discussion, kids may want to move to a different square, which is perfectly acceptable. If everyone agrees, then you'll have the entire group standing on one of the squares, but this is not your goal. The goal is first of all to allow kids the opportunity to think through some of their values and to see them in relationship to the values of others.

7
QUIET GAMES, LIVING ROOM GAMES, AND MIXERS FOR SMALL GROUPS

All of the games in this chapter are designed for use with small groups in confined areas, such as a living room. They require relatively little physical activity and are ideal for parties or for "warm-ups" before a youth meeting.

ANIMAL RUMMY
Give everybody a piece of paper and a pencil. Then, have each person write someone's name at the top of the paper, each letter heading a column:

H	U	B	E	R	T

Everyone should use the same name. The leader now calls "Animal" and each player begins writing the names of as many animals as he can in each column. The animals must begin with the letter at the top of that particular column. Set a time limit and have everyone work on this until the time limit is up (two minutes is usually plenty of time). After they have finished, the leader should ask for all the animals listed in the column and make a master list. Players receive points for each animal they have listed on their sheet, plus a bonus point for each animal not listed by anyone else. This game can also be played with flowers, vegetables, trees, cities, or any other imaginable category.

BANG, YOU'RE DEAD

This is a game where the leader knows the "secret," and the rest of the group tries to guess how it's done. Everyone should be seated around the room in a casual manner, with the leader at the front. After everyone is quiet, the leader raises his hand and points it like a gun, and says, "Bang, you're dead." He then asks the group to guess who was shot. It's hardly ever the person being pointed at. Several people will guess, but they will most likely be wrong. Then you announce who it was that you actually shot.

You do it several times, changing what you do each time to throw people off, but each time pointing a finger at someone and saying, "Bang, you're dead." Make sure that the kids understand that it's possible to know right away who has been shot, but they have to figure out what the "secret" or "clue" is.

And just what is the secret? The person who was actually shot is the first person to speak after you say, "Bang, you're dead." Sooner or later, someone will catch on as you perhaps make it a little more obvious, and that only baffles the rest of the group even more. It's fun as well as frustrating.

BIBLE FAMILY FEUD

Survey your adult Sunday School class to get their answers to the questions listed below. On the surveys, people are asked to give one answer per question. Compile your "survey results," ranking all the answers from most to least common, and use these results in a game of "Family Feud" patterned after the popular television show. It's easiest if you play for games rather than points, like they do on television. Each team sends a player to the front. The question is asked of these two players. The player giving the most common response has the option of "playing" the game or "passing" it to the player of the other team. The team that "plays" the game must name all the responses given (or a maximum of the top six responses) without making three mistakes. If they do, they are the winning team. If not, the other team has a chance to "steal" the game if they can name a correct response not named by the other team. The team winning the most games is the winner.

Possible Questions:
Name a disciple of Jesus.
Name one of the Ten Commandments.
Name a parable of Jesus.
Name a city in Israel.
Name a miracle of Jesus.
Name one of the fruits of the Spirit.
Name one of Paul's letters.

Name one of the plagues of Egypt.
Name a famous Old Testament character.
Name a famous New Testament character.
Name one of the spiritual gifts.
Name a book of the Old Testament.

BOGGLE NAMES

Divide into two groups of four. Each foursome then has its members write their first name in large letters on a single piece of paper underneath each other with a uniform left margin:

Each group plays a game of "Boggle" using the letters in their names. They try to make as many words as they can from the combined letters of the names. Any combination of letters can be used as long as the letters are contingent to each other. (Proper names and foreign words are not permissible.) Set a three minute time limit.

Scoring: One point for two- and three-letter words; two points for four-letter words; three points for five-letter words; five points for words of more than five letters.

BUZZ

For this game, the group should be seated in a circle. Begin counting around the circle from 1 to 100. Whenever someone comes to a number containing a "7" or a *multiple* of 7, he says "Buzz" instead of that number. For example, you would count 1, 2, 3, 4, 5, 6, *buzz*, 8, 9, 10, 11, 12, 13, *buzz*, 15, 16, *buzz*, 18, 19, 20, *buzz*, 22, and so on. You have to stay in rhythm, and if you make a mistake or pause too long, you are out, or you must go to the end of the line.

You can also play "Fizz" which is the same game, except that the number is "5" instead of

"7." That makes the game easier for younger kids. To really get the game complicated, play "Fizz-Buzz," a combination of the two. It would sound like this: 1, 2, 3, 4, *fizz*, 6, *buzz*, 8, 9, *fizz*, 11, 12, 13, *buzz*, *fizz*, 16, 17, 18, and so on.

CHARADES GAMES

The old game of charades is always a winner with small groups in a living room setting. Divide the group in half and have each side think up names or titles for the other side to pantomime. If you want to make sure that the titles are not too hard, think of some ahead of time and put them on small slips of paper into a hat. Each contestant can draw the title they are to charade out of the hat and give it to the other team so that they can see what is being done. Set a time limit of three minutes for each person. Someone should keep time for each side, scoring how long it takes each person to guess the answer. The team with the lowest total time is the winner. Here are some other "charades" variations:

1. Art Charades: This is like regular charades, only each side is given a large drawing pad and a felt-tipped marking pen. Each contestant then *draws* their song, book, or movie title (without using any letters, numbers, or words) and tries to get their team members to guess what they are drawing. This game works well at Christmas time using Christmas carols and songs.

You can make this a fast-moving game by writing about twenty titles on slips of paper and giving the same twenty titles to both teams. Each team has one contestant select a title out of the hat and then draw it on the drawing pad until it's guessed by the team. The next contestant then quickly selects a title, and so on, until all twenty titles have been guessed. The team to guess all twenty titles first is the winner.

2. Valentine Candy Charades: This one, of course, is best for a Valentine's Day party. Get a package of candy "conversation" hearts that have two or three word sayings like "I Love You," "Slick Chick," and "Turtle Dove." Each contestant picks one of the candies from a bowl, and using the regular rules for charades, tries to pantomime the message. Whoever correctly guesses the saying gets to eat the candy. You can use teams or have each person do it for the whole group. It's hilarious to watch kids try to act out phrases like "Lover Boy," "Kiss Me," and all the other crazy sayings on those traditional candies.

3. Occupational Charades: Each contestant in this game of charades tries to pantomime a particular occupation or ambition. Make up a list of creative ones like a rock singer, Miss Universe, an astronaut, a chimney sweep, and an elephant trainer.

4. Hip Charades: This is played just like charades, except that team members spell out words with their *hips* instead of using pantomime or hand signals. Each contestant tries to get their team to guess the words he is spelling out by standing with his *back* to the team and

moving his hips to write the letters in the air. The team shouts out each letter as they recognize it and attempts to guess the correct title in the fastest time possible.

CHOCOLATE BAR SCRAMBLE

Here is a great game for groups of six to ten. Place a chocolate bar in the center of a table. The candy should stay in its wrapper and, to make the game last longer, you could wrap the candy in gift-wrap paper as well. Each person sitting around the table takes a turn at rolling the dice. The first person who rolls a six gets to start eating the candy bar—but ONLY with a knife and fork. And *only* after they put on a pair of mittens, a cap, and a scarf; and *only* after they run once around the table.

While the person who rolled the six is getting ready to eat the candy bar, the group keeps taking turns rolling the dice. If someone rolls a six, then the person who rolled the six before him relinquishes his right to the candy bar, and the second person must try to eat the candy before someone else rolls a six. The game is over when the entire candy bar is eaten or when everyone drops to the floor with exhaustion.

CONFUSION LANE

Have the kids sit in a semicircle. The person on one end takes a pencil and hands it to the person sitting next to him and says, "Here is a pencil." That person says, "A what?" Then the first person must tell him over again. The second person hands the pencil to the third and says, "Here is a pencil." And he says, "A what?" and repeats "A pencil." Then the second person tells the third, "A pencil." This continues all the way around the semicircle. The hard part, however, is that you start a *different* item in the same way from the other end of the line. When they meet in the middle, chaos breaks loose.

CUT THE CAKE

Fill a small bowl with flour packed tightly. Turn it upside down on a television tray or baking sheet, remove the bowl, and leave only the flour mold. Now put a cherry on top. The group gathers around the "cake," and each person takes a knife and "cuts the cake," slicing off any size piece he chooses. The more the cake is cut, the closer each person gets to the cherry on top. Whoever cuts the slice that makes the cherry fall must pick up the cherry with his teeth (no hands) and eat it.

COOTIE

This is a fast-moving game that can be played with as few as four people, works best when you have at least three groups of four. Maximum number for this game is ten groups of four.

Before everyone arrives arrange the tables in a large circle or pattern that will allow movement from a lower number table to the next higher number table. The tables should be numbered consecutively with the No. 1 table considered the highest numbered table. When the group arrives, make sure all the tables are full and remove any extras. Give each person a score sheet and have them write his name on the upper right hand corner of the sheet.

The game is ten rounds long. At the beginning of each round the people sitting across from each other are automatically partners for that round only. The partners then trade score sheets at the beginning of each round to "draw the cootie" for the other while he rolls the dice.

When the game begins, every table starts simultaneously. Each person rolls the dice as rapidly as possible. Each number on the dice corresponds to a part of the cootie's body (see score sheet). A "2" must be rolled first before any other part of the body can be drawn. If a person rolls a number he can use, he keeps rolls until he rolls a number he can't use. Then he passes the dice to the next person. When one person has rolled all the numbers needed to finish his cootie, he may then roll for his partner. When both partners have completed their cooties, they shout, "*Cootie*," and the round is over. Play stops at all tables, regardless of how far along everyone else is.

All partners then trade score sheets and have 60 seconds to add up their score and move to a new table. Movement between rounds is as follows: The people with the highest score at each table move to the next highest numbered table (e.g., from No. 4 to No. 3). People with the lower scores at each table remain at that table. The winners at the No. 1 table remain and the losers at the No. 1 table move to the last table. No one can play with the partner they had in the previous round. The "*Great Cootie*" is the person with the highest total score for all ten rounds.

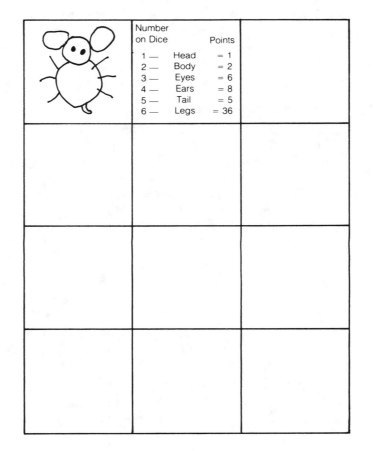

Number on Dice		Points
1 —	Head	= 1
2 —	Body	= 2
3 —	Eyes	= 6
4 —	Ears	= 8
5 —	Tail	= 5
6 —	Legs	= 36

DICTIONARY

Dictionary can be played by any number of people. All that is needed is a dictionary, a pencil, and a 3 x 5 card for each participant. One person finds a word in the dictionary he thinks no one will know the definition of. He asks the group if anyone knows it to make sure no one does. He then copies the correct definition on a 3 x 5 card and asks each participant to write a definition of the word on his card. Each person signs his card.

The definitions are all collected and read to the group, along with the correct one. The object is to guess the correct one. A point is given to each participant who guesses the right definition. A point is also given to each participant for every person who thinks his wrong definition is the correct one. The person choosing the original word is given five points if no one guesses the correct answer.

ELEPHANT, RHINO, AND RABBIT

The players sit in a tight circle with "it" in the middle. "It" points to someone in the circle and says either "Elephant," "Rhino," or "Rabbit." The person to whom he points must either put his hands behind his back for the "Rabbit," put his hands into fists in front of his nose for the "Elephant," or put both fists on his nose with the two index fingers pointing upward for the "Rhino." The two people on either side of the player must put an open hand facing "it" to the first player's head for "Elephant" and a fist to the other's head for "Rhino. For "Rabbit" they must put a fist to the head with one finger pointing upward. All of this must be done before the count of ten. If any one of the three people fail to do his part, he becomes "it."

ELEPHANT   RHINO   RABBIT

DUMB DOLORES

For a good way to acquaint kids who don't know each other very well, have them sit in a circle. One kid says his name and an adjective that begins with the first letter of his name. Some examples are Barfy Bob, Happy Harry, and Awful Alan. The next kid repeats the first kid's "name" and says his own the same way. The game continues around the circle with each one, remembering everybody before him and then himself. These goofy names stick. Later kids remember each other as "Weird Wayne" or "Beautiful Bill" or "Dumb Dolores."

FINGERS UP

Have the kids pair off and face each other with their hands behind their backs. On the count of three, they bring out both hands in front of them with a certain number of fingers held up. They should hold their hands up right in front of their faces so the other person can see them. A closed fist means a zero on that hand. The first person to shout the total number of fingers up on all four hands wins the game. Each pair should go for the best two out of three.

After everyone has done this, all the winners pair off and play the game amongst themselves until there is a championship match between two people.

GEIGER COUNTER

For this game, everyone is seated casually around the room. The leader selects a "volunteer" to leave the room. While he is away, the group agrees on a hiding place for a random object that the leader hides. The person returns and tries to find the object, not knowing what the object is. The rest of the group "tick-tick-tick-ticks" *slower* as he moves away from the object and *faster* as he moves closer until the object is found. Time each contestant to see who can find the object in the fastest time.

GUESS THE INGREDIENTS

Here's a simple "quiz" game to give your kids. Copy the ingredients from a few common items in your pantry or refrigerator. Pass this list out to your kids and have them guess what each item is. Here are a couple of examples:

1. Soybean oil, eggs, vinegar, water, salt, sugar, and lemon juice (mayonnaise).
2. Tomatoes, vinegar, corn sweetener, salt, onion powder, and spice (ketchup).

GUESS WHO

This game helps kids get to know each other better. It's simple and lots of fun. Give each person a 3 x 5 card or paper and a pencil. Have them write down one little-known fact about themselves that probably no one else in the room knows. It can be something like "I was born in Mexico," or "I have on green underwear right now." All statements must be true.

If you have more than twenty people in your group, divide into two teams. Read a "true statement" from one team while the other team tries to guess within ten seconds the identity of the person who wrote it. Each correct guess is worth points.

For smaller groups, number each card and read it to the entire group. Everyone has a pencil and paper and tries to guess who wrote each statement. After all of them have been read, the correct answers are revealed and each person gives himself a point for each correct guess. This can also be done in smaller groups of two or three, discussing each statement and guessing together as a group.

HANDCUFF ESCAPE TRICK

Here's a quick little game that offers a real challenge. Have your kids pair off and give each person a three-foot piece of string. Each couple faces the other and ties the string to their wrists, with one partner's string looped behind the other's so they are linked together. After all are "handcuffed" in this manner, have them try to separate themselves from each other without untying or breaking the strings.

Solution: To escape, pass the center of one partner's string through the wrist loop and over the hand of the other partner (see diagram).

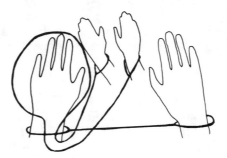

Partner's string
through wrist loop
and over hand

HELP YOUR NEIGHBOR

Here's a fun card game that kids like to play. You need a minimum of four people. You may need to get several games going if there are lots of kids. You will need one deck of numbered playing cards for each four people who play.

Everyone gets cards numbered two through twelve. The cards should be face up in front of each person.

One person in the group rolls a pair of dice. Whatever number is rolled, the player then turns over the corresponding card. For example, if the dice total comes to seven, then the player turns over his number seven card.

The player keeps rolling as long as he has cards to turn over. He can "help his neighbor" by turning over the player's cards to his left to keep his turn alive. His turn continues until he can no longer turn over any cards from either his hand or his neighbor's. The game ends when one person has turned over all of his cards.

HOT POTATO

Most toy stores carry a children's game called "Spudsie," the "hot potato." It's a red plastic potato that you wind up. After about fifteen seconds, a bell inside the potato rings. The object of the game is to pass the hot potato around the group without having the bell ring while it's in your hand. Two rules should be announced: no throwing the potato, and no refusing to accept the potato if it is handed to you. You can play an elimination game, with each "loser" eliminated from the next round. The potato is passed around again and again until a winner is finally declared. The hot potato can also be used to select "volunteers" for other activities.

HOW'S YOURS?

For this game, everyone is seated around the room and a contestant is asked to leave. While that person is out, the group chooses a "noun" like "shoe" or "job" that is to be guessed by the contestant. When the contestant returns, he asks, "How's yours?" to anyone in the room. That person must respond with a true answer, describing the mystery noun that is "his." For example, if the noun is "car," someone might respond with "old" or "expensive." One word adjectives are sufficient. The contestant tries to guess the noun after each adjective given until he guesses correctly. The last person to say an adjective before the correct noun is guessed becomes the new contestant.

INTERROGATION

This is a good get-acquainted activity, especially when you have some new people in the group. It's an especially good game when the youth sponsors are the object of the "interrogation."

Begin by dividing into any number of teams. Each team gets a person to interrogate. The groups are told that the leader has prepared a list of twenty questions such as "What is your favorite food?" or "When is your birthday?" The group, however, doesn't know what those questions are. They have ten minutes to interrogate their person. When the time is up, they are given the questions and must try to answer them. The team that answers the most correctly is the winner.

I NEVER

This game is not only fun but also fosters communication and openness among your young people. Each person is given ten tokens of some kind, such as marbles, matches, or pennies. They must collect other people's tokens by telling everyone "how life has passed you by." Players take turns relating some life experience that almost everyone has had, but they haven't, like ridden a roller coaster. Then, everyone who *has* done this must give a token to that player.

The one rule is that everyone must tell the truth. You may also want to make some rules about good taste. For the most part, this will challenge the kids to do creative thinking and will show that everyone has missed doing something. The person who has missed the most in this game will end up taking home the most.

IRONGUT

If you have some daring kids in your group, try this contest. Prepare a concoction using fifteen to twenty-five ingredients. List *all* the ingredients used. At your meeting, call for some volunteers to be the "Irongut." If teams are already formed, choose one or two from each team.

Those who are brave enough to accept the challenge take turns tasting the potion, which is usually a yucky brown color and thick. The winner is the person who can write down the most correctly identified ingredients. Some suggested ingredients are:

catsup	vinegar
mustard	orange juice
horseradish	tartar sauce
cinnamon	paprika
nutmeg	oregano
garlic	soda
milk	pepper
salad dressing	hot sauce
pickle juice	Worcestershire sauce
onion salt	salt

Keep a careful watch on the kid who asks for seconds!

KILLER

This is a very popular game that your kids will love. Everyone sits in a circle and faces the center. The leader has a deck of playing cards and he lets everyone in the room take one card without showing it to anyone. There are only as many cards in the "deck" as there are people in the room. Whoever draws the "Joker" becomes the "killer." No one, of course, knows who the killer is except the killer himself. Play begins with everyone looking around at each other and talking casually. The killer "kills" people by *winking* at them. When a person notices that he has been killed he *waits ten seconds* and then says, "I'm dead." The object is to guess who the killer is before you get killed. If you guess wrong, then you're dead too. The killer tries to see how many people he can kill before he gets caught. When he *is* caught, the cards are collected, shuffled, and the game can be replayed.

MAD LIBS

Bookstores, novelty stores, and toy stores usually carry a whole series of game books called "Mad Libs." These little books contain funny stories with certain key words omitted, like nouns, adjectives, and persons. The leader asks the group to supply the missing words, not knowing anything about the story. The words should be as ridiculous as possible, and the results are usually hilarious. "Mad Libs" is always a great game for small groups. You can, by the way, write your own.

MAGAZINE SCAVENGER HUNT

Divide your group into teams of two or three persons, give each group a pile of old magazines, and then give them a list of various items, photos, or names that could be found in the magazines. As soon as a group finds one of the items on the list, they cut it out and collect as many as they can in the time limit. The list can be long or short, as difficult or easy depending on the time. The winner is the team with the most items found.

MAP GAME

For this game, get several identical state road maps and draw a large number, letter, or symbol on the map. Make a list of all the towns that the figure crosses or comes near. Have the kids divide up into small groups and give each group a map and the list of towns. On "go" they must locate the towns on the map and figure out what the figure is that the towns form when connected with a line. A wrong guess disqualifies. The first group to find the figure wins.

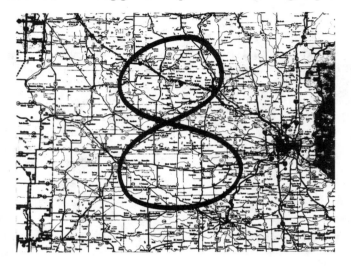

MATCH UP

This is a variation of the television game show "The Match Game." Divide into two or more teams of equal number. Have each team choose a team captain who goes to the front of the room with the other team captain(s). Everyone, including the team captains, should have several sheets of paper and a pencil.

The leader then asks the entire group a question, such as "Who's going to win the World Series this year?" Everyone, without any discussion, writes his answer on a slip of paper and passes it to the team captain, who has also written down an answer. The team captains announce their answers, and a point is awarded to each team for every answer that matches their team captain's. For example, if the team captain answered, "The Dodgers," then his or her team would get a point for every other answer from that team that also was "The Dodgers."

Here are some sample questions:

1. If you were going to repaint this room, what color would you paint it?

2. What country would you most like to visit?

3. What's your favorite television show?

4. What's a number between one and five?

5. What book of the Bible says the most about good works?

6. What's the best way to have fun in this town?

7. What's the funniest word you can think of?

8. How many kids do you want to have?

MIND-READING GAMES

These games are basically alike. There are at least two people who are "clued in" and know how the game is played. The object is for the group to figure out the "secret" that the "mind reader" and the leader is using to perform the trick. As soon as someone in the room thinks they know the secret, he is allowed to see if he can do it. The game can be played until most of the group has figured out the trick or until the secret is revealed.

1. Black Magic: While the mind reader is out of the room, the group picks any object in the room. The mind reader returns, and the leader points to many different objects. When he points to the chosen one, the mind reader correctly identifies it.

Here's how it's done: The chosen object is pointed to immediately after a black object has been pointed to. The name of this game may help give it away.

2. Book Magic: Several books are placed in a row. One of them is chosen for the mind reader to guess when he returns to the room. The leader points to several books at random, and when he points to the correct book, the mind reader identifies it.

Here's how it's done: The chosen book always follows any book pointed to that is on the end of the row.

3. Car: While the mind reader is out of the room, the group picks an object. The mind reader returns and is shown three objects. One of the three is the correct one. The mind reader correctly picks the chosen object.

Here's how it's done: The leader calls the mind reader back into the room with a statement that begins with either the letters "C," "A," or "R." For example, "Come in," "All right," or "Ready." The letter "C" indicates the first object shown; the letter "A" represents the second object; the letter "R" signifies the third object. So, when the mind reader comes back, he knows exactly which object will be the first, second, or third.

4. Knife, Fork, and Spoon Game: In this game, the mind reader leaves the room and the group chooses one person to be the "mystery person." Then, the leader takes an ordinary knife, fork, and spoon and arranges them on the floor in some way. When the mind reader returns, he looks at the knife, fork, and spoon and correctly identifies the mystery person.

Here's how it's done: It actually has nothing at all to do with the knife, fork, and spoon. The leader uses them only as a diversionary tactic. After arranging the knife, fork, and spoon, the leader then takes a seat and sits in exactly the same position as the mystery person. If the mystery person is sitting cross-legged on the floor with one hand on his lap, the leader sits exactly the same way. If the mystery person changes position, so does the leader. The mind reader matches the mystery person with the way the leader is sitting. Meanwhile, everyone is trying to figure out how the knife, fork, and spoon is giving away the clue.

5. Nine Mags: Nine magazines are placed on the floor in three rows of three. The mind reader leaves the room, and the group picks one magazine for the mind reader to identify when he returns. When he does return, the leader, using a pointer of some kind, touches various magazines in a random order, and when he touches the correct one, it's properly guessed.

Here's how its done: The leader touches the first magazine in one of nine possible places:

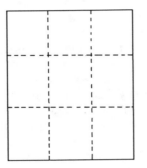

Where the leader puts his pointer on his first magazine determines the location of the selected magazine in the three rows of three. After pointing to the first magazine, the leader then can point to as many others as he wants before pointing to the correct one because the mind reader already knows which magazine it is.

6. Red, White, and Blue: This is just like "Black Magic," only more confusing and almost impossible if you don't know how it's done. The first time the mind reader tries to guess the chosen object, it immediately follows a red object. The next time it follows a white object, and the third time a blue object. It continues to rotate—red, white, blue.

7. Smell the Broom: The leader holds a broom horizontally in front of him, and someone in the group comes up and points to a particular spot on the broom handle. The mind reader enters the room and "smells the broom," sniffing the handle until finally stopping at the correct spot. Everyone thinks that the mind reader has an incredible sense of smell.

Here's how it's done: While the mind reader is smelling the broom, he is really watching the leader's feet. As soon as the mind reader finds the correct spot on the broom handle, the leader raises his foot slightly so that it is undetected by the group.

8. Spirit Move: In this game, the leader holds his hand over the head of a "mystery person" in the room while the mind reader, who is out of the room, correctly identifies that person.

Here's how it's done: Before the game begins, the leader and the mind reader agree on one special chair where the mystery person will sit. When the game begins, Whoever is sitting in that chair will be the first one chosen. Both the leader and the mind reader note this person as instructions are being given to the group. The mind reader then leaves the room. After everyone has moved to new seats, the leader calls to the mind reader and says, "Spirit Moves." He moves his hand over different people's heads until finally stopping over the head of the person who had been sitting in the special chair. The leader then says, "Spirit Rests!" The mind reader identifies the mystery person to everyone's amazement. Then he enters the room to see if he named the correct person, but he is actually looking to see who is *now* in the special chair for the next round.

9. Writing in the Sand: This one is a bit more complicated. The group selects a "secret word" and the mind reader guesses the word after a short series of clues from the leader. The leader holds a stick in his hand and appears to "write in the sand" the clues. The writing neither appears to make sense and nor bears any obvious relationship to the secret word. But the mind reader is still able to guess the word on the first try.

Here's how it's done: Let's use the word "light." The consonants in the word are given to the mind reader through a series of verbal clues after he enters the room. The leader might first say, "Let's see if you can get this one." The first letter of that sentence is "L." That would clue in the mind reader that the word starts with an "L." Then, the leader draws on the floor with the stick, and at some point taps out either 1, 2, 3, 4, or 5 taps. These are the vowels. "A" is one tap; "U" is five taps. The leader would tap three times. Now the mind-reader has two letters. The "G" is given next with a verbal clue like "Got it yet?" As soon as the mind-reader has enough letters to guess the word, he amazes the group by identifying the word.

MY SHIP SAILS

Have everyone sit but the leader who begins the game by picking up a ball and saying, "My ship sails with . . . (and names something that begins with his initials)." For example, if his name is John Doe, he would say, "My ship sails with juicy donuts." He then throws the ball to another player in the room and he too must say, "My ship sails with . . .(?)" If he doesn't know how to play, he will probably say something that doesn't begin with his initials, and he must stand up. He remains standing until he "catches on," and somebody throws the ball to him and he tries again. If he gets it right, he sits down. To start the game, at least two or three people need to know how to play. Explain at the beginning that not everybody's ship sails with the same things. The object is to discover by listening to those who know what their ship sails with what the secret is.

NAME SIX

For this game, have everyone sit in a circle except one person who sits in the center and closes his eyes. An object is passed around until the person in the center claps his hands. The person holding the object at that time must hold the object until the person in the center assigns a letter from the alphabet. The object is then passed around while the person who was caught with the object tries to name six other objects that begin with the assigned letter before the object once again reaches him. If unsuccessful, that person must change places with the person in the center of the circle.

NAME THAT PLACE

This game is great for a small group divided into two teams, or for a larger group split into several teams. Find a book that has pictures or take pictures of a number of recognizable spots in your city. Once the group is divided into teams, hold up a picture for them to see. The group that is first to identify the spot wins a point. The team with the most points wins.

If it's too hard for everyone to see the photos, you could photocopy the pictures or project slides on a screen. The team that identifies the most pictures in a given amount of time wins.

Make sure that you include a wide variety of photos. Have some that are easy to identify, like the city hall or the high school and some that are difficult, like a pond in a certain park or a tree on a street near the church.

NAME THAT SCRIPTURE

This game is a spin-off from the television show "Name That Tune." It can be used at a youth meeting or at a youth group social to test your group's knowledge of familiar Bible passages.

Divide into two teams. The two teams position themselves on opposite sides of the room with the leader standing in the middle. The leader has a list of well-known Bible verses of about ten or twelve words.

Next, the two teams send out one person to compete in the first round. A player "bids" on the first verse. He would say, "I can name that Scripture in six words!" The other player then can say "I can name that Scripture in five words!" The bidding continues until the player stops where he thinks the other player, if he wins the bid, will be unable to complete the verse, or where he will be able to say the verse if he wins the bidding.

If the winning bid is two words, for example, then the leader says the first two words of the verse, and the player must finish the verse correctly. If he is successful, the team gets a point. If unsuccessful, the opposing player gets an additional word and the opportunity to complete the verse. If successful, he gets the point. In other words, whoever wins the bidding gets first chance at winning the point. If the second player doesn't complete the verse correctly, then it goes back to the first player again with an additional word, and so on.

To make the game a bit more risky, the following rule could be used. If you win the bid and cannot complete the verse correctly, the opposing player gets two points if he says it correctly. To make it even riskier, the second player may consult with his team before answering. This insures that the bidding is taken seriously. It's a lot of fun and educational, too!

PASSWORD

Password originated as a television game show and works well for small youth group meetings. Here's how it's played: You need two teams of two. The leader prepares ahead of time a number of words written on 3 x 5 cards that are to be guessed. Any words will do, but nouns generally are best. After deciding which team will go first, the leader shows the secret word (the same word) to both player A's on both teams. Player A on the starting team gives a one word clue to his partner and the partner (Player B) tries to guess the correct word. If he misses, the other team gets a chance. If they also miss, it goes back to the first team, and so on. The best seating arrangement would be something like this:

97

The scoring is five points for a correct guess on the first clue, four points on the second clue, three points on the third clue, and so on. If there is no correct guess after five clues, no points are awarded. However, you can continue and give one point when it is finally guessed. The game ends when one team reaches 21 or any score chosen.

The game can also be played with the entire group at once. For example, if you have eight kids on each team, the seating would look like this:

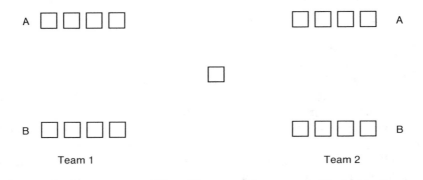

Team 1   Team 2

The leader has each "mystery word" written on a large card. He holds it up so that all the Player A's can see it on both teams, but not the Player B's (and vice versa). The first Player A in each line gives the first clue to the player sitting across from. If this player is unsuccessful, then he moves to the end of the line. The next time their teams get a chance. Two new people try for a correct answer. Other rules stay the same. Alternate each time so the Player A is the clue-giver in one round and Player B is the clue-giver in the next round.

OPEN OR CLOSED

Have the kids sit in a circle and pass around a book or a pair of scissors. When the object is passed, each person announces whether he is passing it "open" or "closed." For example, he might say, "I received it (open or closed) and I am passing it (open or closed). The leader then informs the person whether he is right or wrong. If he is wrong, the leader tells him to sit elsewhere or stand (anything to look conspicuous). The idea is to learn the "secret," which is this: If your *legs* are crossed, you must pass the object *closed*. If your legs are uncrossed, you must pass the object open. It sounds simple, but it really is hard to figure out, which makes for a fun game.

RHYTHM

Everyone in the room numbers off in a circle (1, 2, 3, 4, etc.) with #1 in the end chair. The "rhythm" is begun by #1, and everyone joins in by first slapping thighs, clapping hands, snapping right hand fingers, then snapping left hand fingers in a continuous 1-2-3-4-1-2-3-4-1-2-3-4 motion at a moderately slow speed, which may speed up after everyone learns how to play. The real action begins when #1, on the first snap of the fingers, calls out his own number and on the second snap of the fingers, calls out somebody else's number. For example, it might sound something like this: slap, clap, *"One, six!"* Then #6 might do: slap, clap, *"Six, ten!"* Then #10 would call out somebody else's number on the second finger snap, and so on. If anyone misses, he goes to the end of the numbered progression, and everybody who was after him before moves up one number. The object is to arrive at #1's chair.

An interesting variation of this game is called "Symbol Rhythm." Instead of using numbers, each person uses a symbol like a cough, a whistle, or scratching the head. Rather than calling out numbers, each person does someone else's "symbol"—slap, clap cough, scratch head. Still another version is "Animal Sound Rhythm" that substitutes animal sounds for numbers. Any way it's played, there's a lot of fun.

RING ON A STRING

Have the group sit in a circle on chairs. Have every person hold a piece of string with both hands except for one person who stands in the middle. Tie the string at both ends so it is one large circle with a ring on it that can slide all the way around. Have the group slide their hands along the string and pass the ring along as they try to hide it from the person in the middle. He tries to guess who has the ring by walking around the circle from the inside and tapping different people's hands. When a person's hand is tapped, he opens his hands to reveal whether he has the ring. When the person in the middle taps someone with the ring, they switch places.

S AND T

Divide the group in the middle. Have one side be the "S and T's" and the other side be the "Everything Else's." Everyone counts together as a group from one to twenty, and every time you say a number that begins with an "S" or a "T," the "S" and "T" group stands up. On all the other numbers, the "Everything Else's" group stands up. Start slow, then do it again a little faster. The faster you count, the better the game.

There is an interesting variation of this game. Have everyone sit in a circle and count around the circle, "1, 2, 3, 4," up to 20 and then start at "1" again. Every time a person says a number that begins with an "S" or "T," he must stand up before saying it. If he doesn't, he's out, and the game continues. The counting must be done in rhythm without waiting. It's very confusing, but lots of fun.

THE SITUATION GAME

If you have your group sitting in a circle or in rows, this is a fun game to liven things up. Have each one whisper in the ear of the person to his right *who he is*, being as creative as possible. For example, he is Superman, Donald Duck, or some movie star. Then have each one tell the person to his left *where he is*, such as "in the bathtub," or "on top of a flagpole." Then everybody mixes up and finds new seats, telling the person to the right *what he is wearing* and the person to the left *what he is doing*. After all this, have each person tell who he is, where he is, what he is wearing, and what he is doing, the things the other people told him. For example, "My name is Phyllis Diller; I'm wearing a purple bikini; and I'm in the bathroom, doing push-ups."

SPOONS OR "DONKEY"

This game is similar to musical chairs because someone always gets "left out." Have the group sit in a circle on the floor or around a small table. For "spoons," you will need several spoons and a deck of cards. For each player, you will need four cards of the same suit. The spoons are placed on the floor or on the table equal to the number of players minus one. The cards are mixed up and four cards are dealt to each player. After the players have had a chance to look at their cards, the dealer says "Go," and they start passing one card from their hand to the player sitting on their right. They keep passing the cards around until one player has four of a kind in his hand. He then grabs a spoon, and everyone tries to grab one too. One person will not get a spoon. If the player who first reaches for the spoon does it quietly, then it is often quite a while before the others notice that a spoon is missing, and then they all grab.

This game can be played with coins rather than spoons, and you can call the game "Donkey." Every time someone loses or doesn't get a coin, he gets one letter of the word "Donkey." The first person to lose six times is the donkey. It's a lot of fun.

STATISTICAL TREASURE HUNT

Divide into two teams or into any number of small groups. Give each team or group a list of about twenty items like the ones below. Each team adds up their points based on the information requested. The team with the highest number of points is the winner.

1. Counting January as one point, February as two points, and so on through the calendar year, add up the total of "birthday points" on your team. Simply find out in which month every person on your team was born and add up the points.

2. Counting one point for each different state named, give a score for the different number of states in which your team members were born.

3. Add up the total of all the shoe sizes in your group, one foot only.

4. Add up the total number of operations everyone in your group has had. Serious dental surgery counts but not an ordinary tooth pulling. You must have time to count the number, so there's no time for all the interesting details!

5. Get your "hair color score": black counts two, brown counts one, blond counts three, red counts five, any other color counts seven.

6. Add the total number of miles traveled by each team member from his home to this meeting.

TABLE AND CARD GAMES

There are, of course, dozens of table and card games available in your local department and toy stores that are great for small youth groups. Some favorites include Boggle, Scrabble, Uno, Skip-Bo, Trivial Pursuit, Yahtzee, and Clue.

TAKING A TRIP

Here's a memory game that is always fun. Everyone sits in a circle, and the leader begins by saying, "I'm taking a trip and I'm bringing _____." Anything can be named. The second person then says, "I'm taking a trip and I'm bringing _____ and _____." The *first* item he names is the item named by the first person, and the second is a new item. Continuing around the circle, each person names all the items that have already been mentioned, plus one more that he adds, until someone makes a mistake. Give a prize to whoever can remember the most items in the correct order.

THIRD DEGREE

The leader divides the group into two teams, one composed of FBI members, the other of spies. Each spy is given a card with one of the instructions listed below, but each spy receives a different instruction. The FBI members take turns asking questions of specific spies, calling out the name of each spy before asking the question. They may ask as many questions of as many spies as they choose. They may ask any questions except about the instructions the spies were given. Each spy must answer each question but only in the manner described on his card. Whenever a spy's instruction is guessed correctly by an FBI member, he is eliminated from the game. The questions continue until all the spies' instructions are guessed correctly. If a spy gives an answer without following his instructions, he is eliminated. An FBI member can make a guess at any time, whether or not it is his turn.

The winning spy is the one who has the most questions asked before his instructions are guessed correctly. The winning FBI member is the one who guesses correctly the most instructions.

1. Lie during every answer.
2. Answer each question as though you were (name of adult leader.)
3. Try to start an argument with each answer you give.
4. Always state the name of some color in your answers.
5. Always use a number in your answers.
6. Be evasive—never actually answer a question.
7. Always answer a question with a question.
8. Always exaggerate your answers.
9. Always pretend to misunderstand the question by your answer.
10. Always scratch during your answers.
11. Always insult the questioner.
12. Always begin each answer with a cough.
13. Always mention some kind of food during each answer.
14. Always mention the name of a group member during your answers.

This game can also be played with the entire group. Give everyone an instruction like those listed above. Then have each person answer questions from the entire group until someone can guess his secret instruction. Each new question asked without the instruction being guessed is worth a point.

TOUCH TELEPHONE

This game is based on the telephone game but involves touch rather than hearing. No talking is allowed. Divide the group into teams of about six each. Each team sits in a line, one behind the other. The last person is shown a simple hand drawn picture of an object, such as a house, a cat, or a Christmas tree. Then he tries to draw an exact copy on the back of the person in front of him with his fingers. The drawing can only be done once. The second person draws what he felt onto the back of the person in front of him. Finally the person at the front of the line draws what he felt on a piece of paper. The team whose picture most resembles the original wins that round.

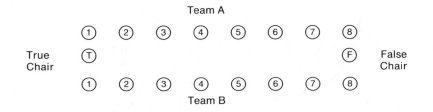

THE TRUE–FALSE SCRAMBLE

Here's a good game to test your kids' Bible knowledge. Two numbered teams sit in opposite rows of chairs. At either end of the rows are the "True" and "False" chairs. The leader makes a Bible-based statement. He can make a false statement, such as "The lunch Jesus used to feed 5,000 plus was five hamburgers and two cokes," or a true one, such as "Jesus said, 'I am the Way, the Truth and the Life.'" After the statement, the leader calls out some numbers. The players with those numbers race for the correct chair. The first one there wins a point for his team. When the players return to their seats, the leader says the correct answer. The team that answers the most questions correctly wins.

TWISTER

This game is available at most toy stores and works well with small groups. It consists of a plastic mat with colored spots and a "spinner" that determines what the players must do. For example, "left hand, yellow" means that a player must put his left hand on a yellow spot on the mat. The next player spins and might get "right foot, red" meaning that he must put his right foot on a red spot. As the game progresses, the players are forced to get into some unbelievable positions. The first person to lose his balance is the loser.

WHO AM I?

Here's an oldie but goodie that is always a lot of fun. On slips of paper write different names of famous people and pin them to the backs of each person, not letting anyone see who they are. Each person is to ask other group members questions that can be answered either "yes" or "no" to help him guess who he is. Kids may only ask one question per person. The first person to guess correctly is the winner; however, the game should continue until everyone has guessed their identities.

WHO SIR, ME SIR?

The object of this game is to work your way up to the "head" chair and stay there. Seat everyone in a semicircle of chairs or benches. Let the group count off; everyone keeps his number for the game no matter where he sits.

The leader begins the action by saying, "The Prince of Paris lost his hat, and number (i.e., eight) knows where it's at. Eight, go foot." Before the leader says "go foot," number eight shouts "Who Sir, Me Sir? or else leaves his seat and goes to the end chair at the leader's right; everyone moves up a seat to fill in his spot.

If he says "Who Sir, Me Sir?" in time, there is a short conversation between the leader and him. Leader: "Yes Sir, You Sir." Number Eight: "No Sir, Not Me, Sir." Leader: "Who then, sir?" Number eight: "Four, Sir" (or any other number). The leader quickly says "Four, go foot," and number four says, "Who Sir, Me Sir?" before the leader finishes. Any time someone goes "foot," the leader starts over with "The Prince of Paris lost his hat."

Teach the group how to play, then start slowly, allowing one mistake each before making anyone "go foot." Then gradually speed up; the faster you go, the more exciting the game gets. Kids like to play this game over and over again.

In case of a tie between the leader and the victim, let the group vote if he should keep his seat or "go foot." With good players you can penalize those who say, "Who Sir, Me Sir?" at the wrong time. Players try to get the ones higher than they out, so they can move up to the head chair. Keep a humorous atmosphere so no one is too embarrassed about going to the foot of the line.

WHOPPER

Here's a fun game that helps people get to know each other better. Each person gets a sheet of paper and a pencil. At the top of the page, he writes four statements about himself. One of the statements must be true; the other three must be false. The true statement should be a "little known fact" that no one would know about until now.

Now the game really begins. One at a time each person reads those four statements, and everyone else tries to guess which one is true. The correct answer is not given until everyone has guessed each time. When it is your turn, you score one point for every incorrect guess When you are guessing about someone else's statements, you get one point if you make a correct guess. At the end of the game, whoever has the most points is the winner. Each person keeps his own score.

You can also play this game in reverse, with each person writing down three true statements and one "whopper." The object then is to guess which one is the lie.

WHY AND BECAUSE

Give everyone in the group a pencil and a 3 x 5 card. Have them write out a question beginning with the word "why." Then have everyone write out answers on cards that begin with "because" and collect them. Redistribute them at random and have kids read the questions they receive along with the answer. The results will be hilarious.

WINK

For this game, arrange chairs facing into a circle. Have each boy stand behind a chair with his hands behind his back. Girls sit in the chairs, except for one chair that is left vacant. The boy behind that particular chair is "it." He must get a girl into that chair by winking at any one of the girls seated in the other chairs. She then tries to get out of her chair without the boy behind her tagging her. If she is tagged, she must remain in her chair, and "it" tries again, either by winking at another girl or the same one. If the girl can get out of her chair without being tagged, she takes the chair in front of "it," and the boy with the vacant chair is now "it." The game continues, and anyone who can avoid becoming "it" is declared the winner. Halfway through the game, have the boys switch places with the girls. If you don't have enough boy-girl couples, pair off any way you choose.

8 ACTIVE INDOOR GAMES FOR SMALL YOUTH GROUPS

All of the games in this chapter are best played indoors in a recreation room. Unlike the games in the prior section, they involve a lot of physical activity and movement. Keep in mind that many of these games can also be played outdoors if you wish, and there are some outdoor games in the next chapter that can be adapted for indoor play.

ALPHABET PONG

For this game, the group arranges itself into a circle. Each person holds a book with both hands. One player takes a ping-pong ball and hits it with the book across the circle, calling out "A." The person on the other side then returns it to someone, calling out "B." The circle works together to see how far through the alphabet they can get. There's no particular order for hitting the ball. Anyone can hit it when it comes to him, but no one may hit the ball twice in a row. For teams, have the first team try it, and then the other. The team to get the farthest through the alphabet without the ball hitting the floor is the winner.

BACK SNATCHING

Here's a mixer with a lot of action. Pin a name onto each kid's back (either phony names, middle names or real names if the kids don't know each other). At a given signal, each person starts copying names from the other kids' backs, while trying to keep people from copying the name on his own back. At the end of the time limit, the person with the longest and most complete list wins.

BACK TO BACK

Divide your group into pairs and have them sit on the floor back to back and link arms. Have everyone stand up. With a little timing and cooperation, it shouldn't be too hard. Then combine two pairs into a foursome. Have the foursome sit on the floor back to back with arms linked. Tell them to stand up. It's a little harder with four. Keep adding more people to the group until the giant blob can't stand up anymore.

BALLOON BURST

Divide your group into two teams and pick a captain for each. Arrange them as diagrammed below. Each team tries to hit the balloon in the direction of its captain, who will then burst the balloon with a pin. One point is scored for each balloon burst. Players must stay seated and use only one hand.

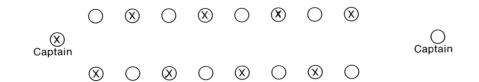

BALLOON GOLF

This game is good in a small game room and also outdoors when there's no wind. First, drop a penny or smooth rock into each round balloon. Then blow the balloon up to about a five or six inch diameter. Golf clubs are made by rolling a full sheet of newspaper into a stick. Cardboard boxes are used as the holes, with the par for each hole written on the side of the box. The weight inside the balloon creates a "mexican jumping bean" effect, causing both difficulty and hilarity for the participants.

BEAN BLITZ

This is a good way to get kids involved with each other at the beginning of a meeting or social event. Each kid is given an envelope containing 20 beans. The kids then circulate around the room asking one person at a time the number of beans in his closed hand. He approaches someone and says "Odd or Even?" If the person guesses correctly, he gets the beans. If he guesses wrong, he must give up the same number of beans. Whoever has the most beans at the end of a time limit wins a prize. When your beans are all gone, you're out.

BILLIARD FLING

If you have access to a billiard table, there are a number of games that are good for small youth groups. The following game is best played on an older table that can take a little abuse. Be sure to protect any windows or lamps in the room.

Set up thirteen balls at random spots on one half of the table. Designate any two balls as the "Fling Balls" that can be handled by the players. Once the game begins, the player may not reach across the cue dot marker on the table to retrieve a Fling Ball.

When the clock starts, the first ball is flung across the cue dot marker at the other balls. The object is to knock all the balls into the top four pockets in the shortest time possible. Any ball rolling back across the cue dot toward the player may be used as a Fling Ball. Balls that pocket on the player's half of the table may be retrieved and used as Fling Balls and do not count as scores.

Scoring is as follows: When all the balls have been knocked into the top four pockets including the Fling Balls, the score is clock's time less thirty seconds. When no Fling Balls roll back to the player's half of the table, the game stops and the score is the clock's time plus ten seconds for every ball left on the table. When a Fling Ball drops into the top pocket without touching another ball, the game stops and the score is the time on the clock plus ten seconds for each ball left on the table.

Give everyone in the group at least one turn, and then have eliminations to determine one winner.

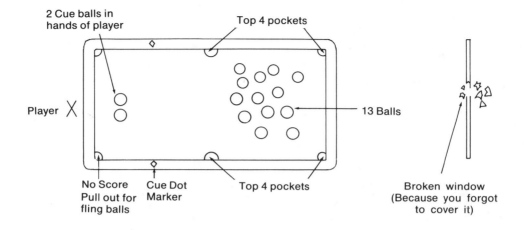

2 Cue balls in hands of player

Top 4 pockets

Player

No Score
Pull out for fling balls

Cue Dot
Marker

Top 4 pockets

13 Balls

Broken window
(Because you forgot
to cover it)

BIRDIE ON THE PERCH

One group forms a circle facing out. The other group forms a circle around the first circle. Pair off—one person from the *inner* circle with one person from the *outer* circle—making partners. At the whistle, the *inner* and *outer* circles move in opposite directions.

When the whistle blows a second time, the people in the *outer* circle kneel on one knee where they are. Their partners from the *inner* circle run from wherever they are and "perch" on their knees. The *last* "couple" to perch is *out*.

The second round begins with the whistle. Circles move in opposite directions. When the whistle blows, the *outer* circle kneels where they are and their partners in the *inner* circle run and perch on their knees. The last couple to perch is *out*. Repeat the rounds until a winning couple is determined.

A good variation of "Birdie on the Perch" is called "Anatomy Shuffle." Like the former game, the group pairs off and forms two circles, one inside the other. One member of each couple is on the inside circle, the other is in the outside circle.

The outer circle begins traveling clockwise, and the inner circle goes counter-clockwise. The leader blows a whistle and shouts something like "Hand, ear!" The inner circle group must find their partners and place their hands on their partners' ears. Last couple to do so is out of the game. The leader calls out various combinations as the game progresses, such as:

"Finger, foot"
"Thigh, thigh"
"Elbow, nose"
"Nose, shoulder"

"Head, stomach"

"Nose, armpit"

The first body member called is always the inner group's part of the body, and they must find their partners, who cannot move after the whistle blows, and touch their part of the body to the second item called on the partner. The last couple to remain in the game wins.

BITE THE BAG

Stand a grocery bag in the middle of the floor and ask everyone to sit in a wide circle around it. One at a time each person must come to the bag and try to pick it up with just his teeth, then return to a standing position. Nothing but the bottoms of his feet are ever allowed to touch the floor. Almost everyone can do this. After everyone has had a turn, cut off or fold down an inch or two of the bag. With each round, shorten the bag more. When a person is no longer able to pick up the bag and stand again, he is out. The winner is the one who can pick it up without falling when no one else can.

BUBBLE HEAD

For this simple game, have two people stand facing each other about four feet apart. Blow up a round balloon and have one player bump the balloon off his head to the other player. The second player bounces the balloon off his head back to the first player. See how many times they can bounce it without dropping it.

The balloon must be hit with the head only. The distance can be varied for greater or lesser difficulty. Each player can move only the left foot while reaching to hit the balloon. No jumping is allowed although each player is allowed to pivot on the ball of his right foot.

A variation of this game is to have teams line up, with players about four feet apart. Each team must bounce a balloon all the way down the team line from one head to the other. Again, right feet must remain planted. If a balloon is dropped, the team must start over again. The first team to succeed is the winner.

CHAIRBALL

This game is an exciting version of basketball that can be played on any open field or large room. Instead of using a regular basketball, use a playground ball or a "Nerf Ball." You may have any number of people on the two teams. At each end of the playing area, have someone standing on a chair holding a wastebasket or a similar container. Like regular basketball, a jump ball starts the game. The players then try to move the ball down the field so that someone on the team can shoot a basket. The person on the chair who is holding the basket may try to help by moving the basket if necessary to try and catch the ball when it is shot. All shots must be made beyond a ten-foot foul line, and the ball may only be moved by throwing it to a teammate or by kicking it. You may not run or walk with the ball. Score baskets like regular basketball, or use any point system that you choose.

√ CHURCH TRIVIA

Divide the group into teams, or kids may compete individually. Give each a list of unusual things in the church to identify. Here's a sample list:
1. The name of the company that manufactured the church's fire extinguisher
2. The number of steps in the baptistry
3. The number of fuses in the fuse box
4. The location of the first-aid kit
5. The last word in a certain book in the church library
6. The number of yellow lines painted on the parking lot

Your list should include twenty or more items such as these. On "go," everyone tries to locate the various information required as quickly as possible. With teams, the questions can be assigned to the different team members. The first to finish answering the most questions correctly wins.

CLOTHES PINNING

Here's another clothespin game that can be played with any size group. Give everyone six clothespins. On "go," each player tries to pin their clothespins on other players' clothing. Each of your six pins must be hung on six different players. You must keep moving, however, to avoid having clothespins hung on you. When you hang all six of your clothespins, you remain in the game, but try to avoid having more pins hung on you. At the end of a time limit, the person with the least amount of clothespins hanging on him is the winner and the person with the most is the loser.

CLOTHESPIN CHALLENGE

This is a simple game for teams of two. Each team must sit in chairs facing each other with their knees touching. Each person is shown a large pile of clothespins at the right of their chair. They are then blindfolded and given two minutes to pin as many clothespins as possible on the pant legs of the other contestant.

Another way to play this is to divide the group into pairs and give each person six clothespins. Each person then tries to hang all his pins on his partner. The winners then pair off again and again until there is a champion clothespinner.

COMIC STRIP MIXER

Take a Sunday paper comic strip that has about 8 or 9 frames to it. Cut it up into its individual frames and pin one frame on the back of each kid in the group. When the game begins, the kids try to arrange themselves in the correct order, so that the comic strip makes sense. Since the frames are on their backs, it means that there will be a lot of communication required.

For larger groups, use several different comic strips (preferably ones that have the same number of frames) and pin them randomly on everyone's back. The game now has the added element of finding others who have the same comic strip. The winning team is the first group to line up with a completed comic strip in its correct order.

CONTEST OF THE WINDS

Draw a large square on the floor. The square is divided into four equal parts, designated as the North, East, South and West. Divide the group into four teams with the same names. Scatter dried leaves or cotton balls evenly in each quarter of the square. At a given signal, the "winds begin to blow," and each team tries to *blow* (no hands allowed) the leaves out of their square into another. Set a time limit and the team with the least leaves or cotton balls in their square wins.

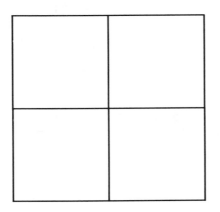

CUP-IT

This game should be played indoors in a large room without carpeting. Break the group into two equal teams. Team A is at "bat" first and sits behind home plate. Team B is in the "field" and is scattered around the room.

A player from Team A must throw a ping-pong ball into the field from no lower than shoulder height. Team B players must attempt to catch the ball with a paper cup in as few bounces as possible. Team A receives a point for each time the ball bounces on the floor before being cupped. Set a maximum number of bounces at 15 due to the dribble effect of the ball just before it rolls. Use a couple of referees to keep track of the bounces. Each member of the team gets one throw, and then the other team comes to bat. Total the points scored every inning, playing as many innings as time will allow.

Here are additional rules:

1. Out of bounds: A line is drawn from left to right through home plate and open doorways. The ball must not be thrown behind the plate or through doorways. Low hanging lights that might obstruct a ball may also be considered out.

2. Throwing: Batting may be in any direction, but when the ball is released, the hand must be above the plane of the batter's shoulder. Fielders may not stand directly in front of the batter or hinder the batter in any way.

DOWN THE DRAIN

For this game, you'll need the plastic tubes found in most golf club bags that protect the clubs. You can probably borrow these from someone. The game won't damage them.

Divide the group into two equal teams. Each team gets half the tubes or one for each player. The teams line up, and the players hold the tubes end to end, using their hands to secure the joints.

At the beginning of each line, the team leaders simultaneously place a marble in the end of the first tube. The team that moves the marble down all the tubes and out the other end is the winner. If the marble slips through one of the joints and falls onto the floor, the team is disqualified. There is some strategy involved, and the kids will really enjoy the challenge.

To make the game a little longer, go for the "best two out of three," or give each team ten marbles to send "down the drain." Only one marble is allowed in the drain at a time. Somebody should be assigned to catch the marbles when they come out.

DUCKIE WUCKIE

Everyone sits in a circle with one person standing in the middle. The person in the middle is blindfolded and has a rolled up newspaper. He is spun around as everyone else changes seats.

Everyone needs to be silent. The person blindfolded then finds a person's lap only by means of the end of the newspaper. Once a lap is found, the newspaper is unfolded and placed on the lap. The blindfolded person sits on the newspaper and says "Duckie Wuckie." In a disguised voice the person being sat upon responds with "quack-quack." After each "quack-quack," the blindfolded person may guess the identity of the voice. "Duckie Wuckie" and "quack-quack" may be repeated twice. If correct, the person who says "quack-quack" gets the blindfold, if incorrect the blindfolded person must find another lap and try again.

ELECTRIC FENCE

To begin, you need two poles and a piece of rope or string. The rope is tied between the two poles, about two feet off the floor.

Divide into teams. The object of the game is for the entire team to get over the "electric fence" (the rope) without getting "electrocuted"(touching the rope).

After each successful try, the rope is raised a little higher. Eventually, teams will be eliminated as they find the rope too high to get over.

What makes this game interesting is that even though only one player goes over the rope at a time, the other team members can help in any way they want. Once a person is over the fence, however, he must stay over the fence and not come back around to help anyone else. The last person must somehow get over the fence without help on one side. This game requires teamwork.

Teams can be eliminated entirely if one person touches the fence, or elimination can be done on an individual basis. Make sure your teams are evenly divided according to height, age, and sex.

FICKLE FEATHER

Lay a sheet flat on the floor. Have all the kids kneel around all four sides of the sheet and then pick it up by the edges. They pull it taut and hold it under their chins. A feather is placed on the sheet, and the kids try to blow the feather away from their side. Each side of the sheet is a team, and if the feather touches one of the team members or gets blown over their heads, that team gets a point. The team with the fewest points is the winner.

FLEA MARKET

Prepare ahead of time a large number of one-inch square pieces of paper, all different colors. These are hidden all around the room. Some squares have numbers on them. At a starting signal, the entire group hunts for the squares, and as soon as they have been found, kids start trading with each other, trying to acquire the colors that they think are worth the most. The real value of the colors and numbers are unknown to the players until the trading is over. Then announce the values and whoever has the most points wins. This game can also be an Easter Egg Hunt.

Colors: White = 1 point
Brown = 5 points
Green = minus 5 points
Blue = 2 points
Red = 10 points

Numbers: 7 = add 50
11 = double score
13 = subtract 50
15 = add 1
etc.

FOURSQUARE

Foursquare is an old playground game that works well with small youth groups, indoors or out. To play, you need to draw a sixteen-to-twenty-foot square on the floor, divided into four equal sections:

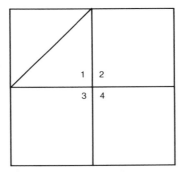

Four players stand in boxes 1 through 4 and the remaining players line up outside #4. Player #1 is always the server. He hits the ball underhand to one of the other squares after first bouncing it in his own square once. The receiver then tries to keep it in play after it has bounced once in his square by hitting it underhand to a square other than to the the one from which he received it. Play continues after each serve until someone commits one of the following fouls:

a. Failing to return the ball after it bounces once.
b. Hitting the ball out of the square.
c. Hitting the ball back to the person who hit it to him.
d. Hitting the ball with his fist or downhanded.
e. Stepping over the server's line on a serve.
f. Playing in someone else's square.
g. Allowing the ball to touch your body.
h. Holding the ball.

The person who commits the foul leaves the game and lines up in back of the line (square #4). All players move up. The object of the game is to get into the server's square and stay there as long as possible.

FRUITBASKET UPSET

This game can be played with any number of people. The group sits in a circle of chairs, with one less chair than there are people. The extra person stands in the middle. Everyone is secretly assigned the name of a fruit. The person names several fruits, then he yells "Go." Those people who were assigned the fruits named must change chairs. At the same time, the person in the middle also tries to get one of the vacant chairs. The person who fails to get a chair is then the one in the middle and repeats the game. As an option, the person in the middle may call out "Fruitbasket Upset" at which time everyone must exchange chairs. Be sure to use sturdy chairs. This game usually ends with people landing in other people's laps.

HAND OVER HAND

Divide your group into one or more teams of five. Each team forms a circle and everyone holds his right hand in the middle of the circle. Have them stack their hands "basketball huddle style." Then have them place their left hand in the circle in the same manner so that left hands are stacked on top of the right hand stack. At the signal, the person whose hand is on the bottom should take that hand and place it on top of the stack. The next person should do the same, and so on until the person who began the process is again on the bottom. The first team to complete this process is winner of round #1. For the next round try three "laps." Then try five. After everyone has learned the game, try going backwards.

HUMAN TIC-TAC-TOE

As suggested by its title, this game is played just like it is on paper, except that people are used. It's very active and great for smaller groups. To play, set up nine chairs in three rows of three. Team One stands on one side of the chairs and Team Two on the other. Players on each team then number off.

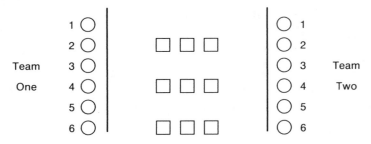

The leader then calls out a number, like "4." As soon as the number is called, the two "4's" on each team scramble to sit down in any two chairs as quickly as they can. When they are seated, another number is called. The game continues until three teammates from either team have successfully scored a "tic-tac-toe." If no tic-tac-toe is made, then the players return to their team, and the game is played again.

A variation is to play with ten people per game. They all take a seat in one of the nine chairs, leaving one person without a seat. When the whistle is blown, everyone must move to a different chair, while the "extra person" tries to sit down somewhere. After the mad scramble for seats, the game is scored like tic-tac-toe. Any row of three people from the same team gets points. Each round, there will always be one person left without a seat.

An even crazier way to play this game would be to play as described above, but use guys on their hands and knees as "chairs" and have girls from each team sit on the guys' backs. When the whistle is blown, they jump on a guy and try to hang on, even though another girl may try to pull her off or take the same guy. It's really wild. Whether you use chairs, guys, or lines on the floor, it's a lot of fun to play.

INDOOR SCAVENGER HUNT

Divide the group into two or more teams. Each team gets into one corner of the room. You stay in the middle of the room. Each team appoints a "runner" who runs items from the team to you. You call out various items that might be in the group, and each team tries to locate that item among team members, then gives it to the runner. He runs it to you. The first team to produce the named item wins one hundred points, and after twenty or more items, the team with the most points wins. Make sure that the runners are all running approximately the same distance. Here are some sample items:

A white comb	A shoestring (without the shoe)
A red sock	Four belts all tied together
A 1969 penny	The smallest sock you can find
A student body card	(judge to decide the winner)
An eyelash curler	A picture of your mother
A white T-shirt	Forty-six cents exactly
Dark glasses	A handkerchief
Picture of a rock star	A cowboy boot
A twenty dollar bill	
A stick of gum	
A theater ticket	
A blue sweater	
Toenail clippers	
A book of matches	

INDOOR SOCCER

Clear out an open space on the floor, and have everyone get down on their hands and knees. There should be two teams. Goals should be marked on both ends of the room. A feather or a ping-pong ball is placed between the two teams, and the players try to *blow* the feather or the ping-pong ball across the other team's goal line. No hands are allowed. There should be no more than five or six kids on a team.

INDOOR VOLLEYBALL

You can play an exciting volleyball game inside, even with a low ceiling, by using a "Nerf" basketball. Hang up a regular net, drape sheets across a rope or stack up tables between the two teams. For low ceilings, keep the net low and have everyone play while sitting on the floor or on his knees. Other volleyball rules apply.

INVERSION

This game requires teamwork. It can be played as a competitive game or as a cooperative game.

Draw two parallel lines on the floor about eighteen inches apart. The team lines up inside those two lines. They number off from one end of the line to the other.

18" ① ② ③ ④ ⑤ ⑥ ⑦ ⑧ ⑨ ⑩ ⑪ ⑫ ⑬ ⑭

On a signal, they must reverse their order without stepping outside those two parallel lines. For example if there are 20 people on the team, then player #1 must change places with player #20. Only the person in the middle stays in the same place.

Let the teams practice once and find a strategy for changing places quickly and accurately. Then compete against the clock and try to set a "world record" or see which team can do it in the quickest time. Referees can penalize a team in seconds lost when a person steps outside one of the two lines.

LET IT BLOW

Divide your group into teams and give each person a deflated balloon. At the signal, the first person on each team blows up his balloon and lets it go. The balloon will sail through the air. That person must then go to where it lands, stop and blow it up again, and let it go. The object is to get the balloon across a goal line some distance away. When he does, he can run back and tag the next player on the team, and then that person must do the same thing. This game is really fun since it's almost impossible to predict where the balloons will land each time. It's especially fun and interesting when played outside because the slightest breeze blows the balloon in a different direction. The goal line should be about fifteen feet away.

LONGJOHN STUFF

This is a hilarious game that is always fun with any group. You will need two pairs of long underwear, about one hundred six-inch-round balloons, and a straight pin. Divide into two teams. Each team selects one person from their team to put on a pair of longjohns over his clothes. It would be best for them to pick someone who is not too big. Each team also selects two or three "balloon stuffers."

When the kids are ready, throw out an equal number of balloons to the two teams. The team members must blow them up all the way, tie them, and pass them to the "stuffers" who try to

121

stuff all of them into the longjohns. The object is to see which team can stuff the most balloons into their person's longjohns within the given time limit, usually about two minutes. Stop the two teams, and have the two people in the longjohns stand still. Now would be a good time for some pictures.

To count the balloons, begin with the one who appears to have the fewest balloons, and pop them with a pin through the longjohns while the team counts.

MAD ADS

This game is similar to Indoor Scavenger Hunt, described previously. Divide into teams and give each team the same issue of the same magazine. Ahead of time, the leader lists about thirty or forty big and small advertisements in the magazine.

Instruct the teams to tear the pages out of the magazine and divide them up between the team members. They can spread them out on the floor if they want. The leader stands an equal distance from all the teams and calls out the name of an advertisement. The first team to locate the ad hands it to their "runner," who takes it to the leader, and the team wins a designated number of points. The team scoring the most points wins.

Here are a couple tips: If one team is slaughtering the others, increase the point value of ads later in the game so that the other teams can have a chance to catch up. Women's magazines are best for this game because they seem to carry more ads than most magazines.

MAD HATTER

Here's a free-for-all game that is really wild. Everybody needs a cap or hat of any kind. If you want the game to last longer, use ski caps. Give everybody a "club," a sock stuffed full of something soft. When the signal to begin is given, everybody tries to knock off everybody else's cap while keeping his own on. No hands may be used to protect yourself or your cap, and you may not knock off anyone's cap with anything except the sock club. When your cap is gone, you are out of the game. See who can last the longest.

MARSHMALLOW PITCH

Have your kids pair off and give each pair a sack of miniature marshmallows. Each pair should also have a neutral "counter." One person is the pitcher; the other the catcher. On "go," the pitcher tosses a marshmallow into the catcher's mouth, and the catcher must eat the marshmallow. The pitcher and catcher should be about ten feet apart. The counter counts how many successful catches are made. The couple who catches the most at end of a time limit or who catches twenty first is the winner.

MUSICAL BACKS

This is similar to musical chairs and other elimination games. Kids are to mill about the room, and when the music stops or the whistle blows, everyone must quickly find another person and stand back to back. When there are an odd number of people on the floor, someone will not have a partner, and he is eliminated from the game. When there is an even number of people playing, a chair is placed in their midst, and anyone may sit in it and be safe. Every other round, the chair will need to be removed. Make a rule that everyone must keep moving and players may not pair off with the same person twice in a row. The last person to survive wins. It's a lot of fun.

MUSICAL GUYS

This game is played exactly like musical chairs, except guys are used in the place of chairs. The guys form a circle, facing the center on their hands and knees. The girls (there should always be one more girl than the number of boys) stand behind the guys and at the start of the "music," the girls begin walking clockwise around the guys. When the music stops, the girls grab any guy and jump on his back "horsey" style. The girl without the guy is out. The girls should be encouraged to "fight" for their guy. Play again with one less girl and one less guy in the circle. The last girl is the winner.

MUSICAL COSTUMES

Here is a fun game that allows everyone to look a little silly. Before you start, have a laundry bag or pillow case filled with various articles of clothing—funny hats, baggy pants, gloves, and belts. Keep the bag tied shut so the clothing won't spill out.

Have your group make a circle and start passing the bag around as music is played. When the music stops, the person "holding the bag" must reach in and take out an article of clothing without looking. Then he must put it on and wear it for the remainder of the game. Try to have enough so that each person gets three or four funny articles of clothing. This can lend itself to seasonal clothing, such as Santa's bag or Easter Parade hats. It may also be a fun way to create an instant "costume" for a Halloween party. After the game, you can have a fashion show or take pictures to hang on the group's bulletin board.

MUSICAL HATS

Pick six guys to stand in a circle, each facing the back of the guy in front. In other words, they would all be looking clockwise, or counter-clockwise. Five of the guys must put on hats or paper paint buckets. When the music starts, each guy grabs the hat on the person's head in front of him and puts it on his own head. The hats move around the circle from head to head until the music stops. Whoever is left without a hat is out of the game. Remove one hat and keep playing until there are only two guys left. They stand back to back, grabbing the hat from each other's head, and when the final signal is given, the one wearing the hat is the winner.

NERF BASEBALL

Here's how to play baseball indoors with a small group. All that is needed is a "Nerf" baseball, a "Whiffle" bat, and a room large enough for the bases. The bases are placed twenty-five feet apart and they are one-and-a-half foot squares made from masking tape. The pitcher's mound is about fifteen feet from home plate. All the rules are the same as regular baseball except that the runner can be put out if he isn't on the base and is hit by the Nerf Ball.

NERFKETBALL

Here is a fun variation of basketball using a "Nerf" basketball or soft sponge and a few chairs. Choose two teams of equal number and seat them alternately on sturdy chairs as shown in the diagram: two rows of players facing each other. For best results, players should be spaced at least double arm's distance apart both sideways and across. Place a small bucket for the "basket" on the floor at the end of each double row, approximately six feet from the players at the ends of the rows.

Here are the two ground rules: (1) Chairs cannot be moved or tipped. (2) Each player must remain seated while the ball is in play.

Flip a coin, and decide which team will take first possession of the ball. Play begins when the referee gives the ball to the player farthest from his team's goal. The team tries to work the ball toward their goal by passing it while opponents try to block passes and steal the ball. Any player may take a shot at the goal at any time, but the advantage of passing the ball to the player nearest the goal is obvious. If the ball is intercepted by the other team, play continues in the opposite direction.

When an attempted field goal misses, the ball is automatically "out" to the other team, and play goes the other way. When a field goal is scored, all players rotate one seat to the right. This will give each player the opportunity to be his team's prime shooter during the game. After rotation, the ball goes "out" to the other team.

Any ball loose within the playing area is a free ball. Any ball going outside the playing area is given to the player nearest the last player to touch the ball.

Penalties may be assessed, and free throws are awarded for players leaving their seats or showing unnecessary roughness. Limit the game either by using a kitchen timer for quarters and halves or by setting a scoring limit.

PAPER SHOOT

Divide into teams of four to eight. Set a three-foot garbage can in the middle of the room. Prepare ahead of time several paper batons and a lot of wadded up paper balls. One team lies down on their backs around the trash can with their heads toward the can. Each of these players has a paper baton. The opposing team stands around the trash can behind a line approximately ten feet away from the can. This line can be a large circle drawn around the can. The opposing team tries to throw wadded up paper balls into the can, and the defending team tries to knock the balls away with their paper batons while lying on their backs. The opposing team gets two minutes to shoot as much paper as possible into the can. After each team has had its chance to be in both positions, the team that has the most paper balls in the can is the winner. To make the game a bit more difficult for the throwers, have them sit in chairs while they toss the paper.

PING-PONG BASKETBALL

This game can be played individually or in teams but is best played on a hard floor. It's simple and fun. Set up a large number of different-sized containers around the room and assign each one a point value. The larger the container, the lower the points. Then, have kids try to bounce ping-pong balls into the containers for points. The ball must bounce at least once before it goes into a container.

PING-PONG VARIATIONS

Ping Pong is an old stand-by for small youth groups, but there are some interesting versions of the game that make it even more challenging.

1. Round Table Ping Pong: Up to approximately twenty persons may play. One person picks up a paddle at each end of the table. Other players line up behind these two facing clockwise around the table. One person serves, drops the paddle on the table, and moves around the table clockwise as the next person picks up the paddle and returns the ball. Continue rotating until someone misses. The player who misses is out of the game.

2. Spool Pong: This is played like regular Ping Pong, except that you place two spools, one on each side of the net, on the center line of the table about eighteen inches from the ends of the table. Place an extra ping-pong ball on top of each. Add five points to your score if you can knock your opponents ball off the spool. Otherwise score the game normally.

3. Water Pong: Fill two small saucers full of water and place one on each side of the net about twelve inches from the net and on the center line. If your opponent hits the ball in your saucer, he wins the game. Score the game normally unless it ends with a ball in the saucer.

POOPDECK

To set up this game, clearly mark off three sections on the floor with tape or chalk. One section is the "poopdeck," one the "maindeck," and the last the "quarterdeck." Begin with everyone standing in the poopdeck area. Call out the name of a deck including where they are standing and the kids run to the deck you have called. The last person on the deck is out. If the kids are in "poopdeck" for example, and you call out "poopdeck," any kid who leaves the poopdeck is out. The game continues rapidly until one person is the winner.

POOPDECK	MAINDECK	QUARTERDECK

To challenge your kids give them a few trial runs to warm up and new kids a chance to learn the game, call the decks loudly and distinctly, then point to the opposite deck that you call.

RAINBOW SOCCER

This game is played with two teams and sixty balloons (thirty each of two colors). The balloons are mixed together and placed in the center circle of a regulation basketball court.

The two teams line up on the end lines facing each other. One person from each team is the "goalie" and stands at the opposite end of the floor in front of a large container.

At the whistle, using soccer rules each team tries to kick their balloons to their goalie, who then puts them into the container behind him. To play defense, a team stomps and pops as many of the other team's balloons as possible. Play continues until all the balloons are scored or popped. The team with the most goals wins.

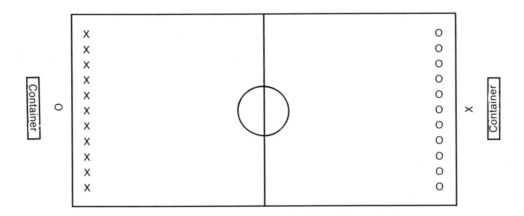

SANCTUARY SOCCER

This version of soccer allows you to play indoors and has a built-in equalizer to keep one team from dominating the game.

Play in a large room with all the chairs removed. You will need a Nerf soccer ball and eight folding chairs. Line up four chairs at each end of the playing area for goals. Play regular soccer with as many players as you wish. A goal is scored when the soccer ball hits one of the other team's chairs.

When points are scored, the chair that is hit is removed. Before the first goal, for example, the setup would look like the diagram at the top of the next page.

After team "B" scores a goal, the setup would look like this:

The team that was just scored on will have an easier, larger target when the ball is back in play, while the other team has a smaller, more difficult target. Each team can have one goalie, as in regular soccer.

SHUFFLE YOUR BUNS

Here's a fun game you can play over and over again. Arrange chairs in a circle so that there will be two extra chairs in the circle. Each person sits in a chair except for two people in the middle who try to sit in the two vacant chairs. The people sitting in the chairs keep moving from chair to chair to prevent the two in the middle from sitting down. If one or both of the two in the middle manage to sit in a chair, the person on their right replaces them in the middle of the circle and then tries to sit in an empty chair.

SNOWFIGHT

This is a snowball fight without snow. Instead of snow, use wadded up newspapers. Divide into two teams and separate them with a row of chairs or some other boundary. Give each team a stack of old newspapers. Teams get three minutes to wad them up into balls. When the signal to "go" is given, they try to throw all of their paper into the other team's territory. After the time is up, the team with the least amount of paper on its side is the winner. You can play several rounds. After the game, have a paper-cleaning-up contest to see which team can gather up the most paper and stuff it into trash bags.

SOCCER ON PAPER

Here's a new way to play soccer that is best played indoors. It's like regular soccer, except that you give each person, including the goalie, a piece of paper to stand on and a particular place to put the paper. He must keep one foot on the paper at all times. "Scooting" the paper is not allowed. Be sure to scatter players of both teams evenly all over the playing area. Toss in a soccer ball, and the effect is like a giant pinball machine.

STEAL THE BACON

Two teams line up behind two lines about twenty feet apart. Team members should number off. A blanket, the "bacon," is placed between the two teams in the center. The leader calls out a number, and the two people on each team with that number run out and try to pull the "bacon" back across their team's line, which scores a point for the team. On occasion, the leader can call out more than one number.

TECHNICOLOR STOMP

Here's an indoor game that uses lots of colored balloons. Divide the teams and assign each team a color. Then give each team an equal number of balloons of their color. They blow up all the balloons and tie them. When the game begins, the balloons from all the teams are released onto the floor, and the object is to stomp on and pop all the balloons of the other teams while attempting to protect your own team's balloons. After two to three minutes, the popping stops, and each team gathers up its remaining balloons. The team with the most balloons left is the winner.

THREAD THE NEEDLE

For this game you will need two table knives that have a "neck" between the blade and the handle and two balls of medium-weight string.

Divide the group into two teams. Each kid starts at exactly the same time to thread the "needle," which is the knife, with the end of the string tied tightly to the neck of the knife down through his shirt and one pants leg or comparable clothing. This person then passes the "needle" on to next person on his team. Each team member is continually feeding "thread" along the way so that there is enough thread to connect the entire team.

When the last guy has "threaded the needle," he then begins the process of "unthreading the needle!" This is done by pulling up on the string and getting the "needle" up, through, and out of his slacks and shirt. When "unthreading the needle," each team member works to pass the slack in the string along. In the end, the first person in line has the string in a neat ball again, and the team has not "unthreaded " the needle at any given time!

TOUCH

This game is easy to play indoors or out. The kids first line up in some predetermined order, such as alphabetically. Then, the leader names some object that everyone can see. All the kids run and touch it, and then get back in their place in line. The last person to get back in line is out of the game. Any object can be used, including something that one person is wearing, such as "Dick's right shoe!"

TOWEL THROW

For this game, the group is seated in chairs, preferably in a closed circle. One person stands inside the circle. The group passes or throws a towel around the circle to anyone in the circle. The kid in the middle then tries to tag the person who has the towel. When he catches somebody with the towel, they exchange positions. If he catches the towel in midair, the kid who threw it has to become "it."

TRASH CAN BASKETBALL

This is an indoor version of basketball. Set up large trash cans at each end of the room. Use a soft, children's ball about eight inches in diameter. Rules are the same as normal basketball except for a few:

1. There is no dribbling. All movement of the ball is by passing.

2. No running with the ball.

3. If you touch a player with the ball, that's a foul. The fouled player gets a free shot.

4. There should be a ring drawn about six feet out around the trash cans, in which no one is allowed.

TRIPLE THREAT BASKETBALL

Here's a crazy way to play basketball. It requires one basket and three teams. You can have three teams of any size; however, a maximum of five players and a minimum of two would be best. The rules of the game are similar to regular basketball, but with these changes:

1. Baskets are worth one point. The game is played until one team has ten points and is leading the other two teams by at least two points each.

2. After each basket is scored, the team in last place is awarded the ball out of bounds, even if they were the team that just scored. In the event that more than one team is tied for last, the team that has had the low point total the longest is awarded the ball.

3. In the event that play is stopped for some reason other than a basket, such as the ball going out of bounds, traveling, or double dribble, the team in last place is again awarded the ball. If the last place team were guilty of the violation, the ball is given to the team that is next to last.

4. In the event of a foul, the team that was fouled takes the ball out of bounds. There are no foul shots.

This game can be played with two baskets on a regular basketball court. Teams "rotate" baskets after each goal is scored. Part of the fun is trying to remember which basket is yours. Another version would be to play with four teams and four baskets on each side of a square, if you have baskets that can be moved. You could, of course, play the game with a Nerf ball and cardboard boxes or trash cans for baskets. Be creative and have fun!

UNDERDOG

This game should be played in a large, open space. Choose one player to be "it." "It" then tries to tag the other players, who must "freeze" when they are tagged. Frozen players may be unfrozen by standing with their legs apart and allowing a free player to go between their legs. "It" tries to freeze all the free players and when he does, the game is over. Allow several kids to be "it." For larger groups, make several players "it" at the same time.

9 OUTDOOR GAMES FOR SMALL YOUTH GROUPS

All of the games in this chapter are best played outdoors on an open field, in someone's backyard, or at a camp or retreat. For more outdoor games, use any of the relays in Chapter 10 or adapt some of the indoor games in the previous chapter for outdoor use.

BUCKET BRIGADE

For this game, you need two teams. Each team lines up single file with a bucket of water on one end and an empty bucket on the other. Each team member has a paper cup. The object of the game is to transfer the water from one bucket to the other by pouring the water from cup to cup down the line. The first team to get all of its water to the empty bucket is the winner.

CRAZY BASEBALL

This version of baseball can be played with any size group by by changing the "foul lines," moving them closer together for small groups or farther apart for large groups.

Divide the kids into two teams. The ball should be a partly deflated volleyball, and the bat is a regular baseball bat. There are only two bases—home plate and first base. First base can be as far away from home plate as you choose. The team up at bat pitches to itself. Batters only get one pitch, and they must swing. If they miss the ball entirely, they are out. Two foul balls or fly balls that are caught constitute outs. As soon as the ball is hit, the batter runs to first base. The fielding team can get a force out at first or hit the runner with the ball.

When the batter gets to first base, he does not have to come home until it's safe to do so. In other words, the team at bat could put five or six people on first base at the same time. Then, when a ball is well-hit, all five people can score a run at once by running for home plate.

The fielding team can play all over the field. There are no "positions" except first base and catcher. As soon as there are three outs, the team in the field can run immediately up to home plate and start hitting. They don't have to wait for the other team to get ready in the field.

Batters should line up at home plate boy-girl-boy-girl, and then number off so they can get in the same batting order each time.

If you want to make sure everyone gets an "at-bat" every inning, allow more "outs" per inning or make the "outs" meaningless, except for preventing runs. Change the rules and adapt the game to fit the needs of your group.

CENTIPEDE RACE

This game can be played indoors or out. All you need are benches. Seat as many kids on each bench as possible, straddling it like a horse. When the race starts, everyone must stand up, bend over, and pick up the bench, holding it between their legs. Then they run like a centipede. The finish line should be forty to fifty feet away. It's a lot of fun to watch.

CROWS AND CRANES

Divide the group into two teams. One side is the "Crows," and the other is the "Cranes." The two teams are lined up facing each other on two lines four or five feet apart. The leader flips a coin and calls out the name of the team that won the toss. If the leader calls "Crows," the "Crows" must turn around and run, with the "Cranes" in hot pursuit. If any of the "Cranes" succeed in touching a member(s) of the "Crows" before he crosses a given line about twenty to sixty feet away, he is a captive of the "Cranes" and must aid the "Cranes" when play continues. The team that captures all the members of the other team is the winner.

DAVID AND GOLIATH

Divide the group into teams, for example, "David I" and "David II," with the same number of guys and girls on each team. Each team is given one old nylon stocking and one whiffle ball to place in the toe of the nylon. One person of the same sex from each team steps forward to the throwing line. Each twirls the nylon over his head or at his side and sees who can throw it the farthest. The winner gets one point for his team. The team with the most points wins the contest. Then repeat this contest for accuracy. Set a "Goliath" (a person, chair, or other object) approximately thirty feet from the throwing line. The person who comes the closest to hitting "Goliath" gets one point for his team. If he should hit "Goliath," an additional bonus point is awarded to the team. The kids will quickly find out that it took practice for David to be such a skilled marksman.

FOOTBALL VARIATIONS

You can play regular football with small youth groups, but these variations of football usually make the game more fun for coed groups:

1. Jungle Football: This is essentially touch or flag football, but all players are eligible to catch a pass. The "quarterback" or ball carrier can also run across the line of scrimmage and still pass the ball forward or backward to another player. Multiple passes on one play are allowed. Each team gets four downs to score. There are no first downs. Only touchdowns are counted (six points), and safeties (two points).

2. Bombs Away: This version of football is very simple. After the ball is hiked, everybody goes out for a pass. No rushing the quarterback is allowed. Everyone is a wide receiver on the offensive team, and everyone is a defensive back on the defensive team. The quarterback can take as long as he wants to throw the pass. There is no running with the ball after it is caught. After a completed pass, the next play is from that point on the field. Players must rotate the quarterback position so that everyone gets to be the passer. A touchdown is scored when a pass is completed into the end zone.

3. Flamingo Football: This is tackle football with the boys against the girls; however, the boys must play the entire game hopping on one foot whenever the ball is in play. The girls usually clobber the guys.

FRISBASKETBALL

Next time your group wants to play basketball, why not try this game. Instead of a basketball, use a Frisbee and any number of players on a regular basketball court. Of course, you can't dribble a Frisbee, so you must advance it by passing. The refs should call penalties, such as fouls, traveling and "out of bounds" just as they normally would in a basketball game. Points should be awarded as follows: one point for hitting the backboard, two for hitting the square on the backboard, and three for making a goal (including foul shots). Double the scores for any shot made from behind half-court.

GOLF GAMES

Golf is a great outdoor game for small groups, but most young people aren't too good at it. Here are some variations of the sport, adapted for youth groups:

1. Croquet Golf: This is actually miniature golf played with a croquet set. The wickets are used instead of cups in the ground. Set up your own nine hole course by arranging the wickets around the yard. Try to make each hole different by having to go around objects such as shrubs, through tin cans and tires, and up ramps and hills. Tag each wicket with the hole number as well as placing small signs at each tee where the players must begin each hole. Indicate how many strokes will be par for each hole on the tee sign along with the hole number. Some croquet sets include wicket tags and tee signs for playing croquet-golf.

2. Frisbee-Golf: Lay out a short golf course around the area using telephone poles, light posts, fence posts, tree trunks, and the like, for "holes." You can set up places as the tees or designate a certain distance from the previous "hole, " such as ten feet for the starting place. Each person needs a Frisbee. The object of the game is to take as few throws as possible to hit all the "holes." Each person takes his first throw from the tee and then stands where it landed for his next throw until he hits the "hole." Of course, discretion must be used when the Frisbee lands in a bush or tree. One penalty "throw" is added to the score if the Frisbee can't be thrown from where it lands. The course can be as simple or as complicated as the skill of the participants warrants. Such obstacles as doglegs, doorways, arches, and narrow fairways add to the fun of the course.

3. Golfennis: This is simply a golf game using tennis balls instead of regular golf balls. Provide the kids with plenty of tennis balls, golf clubs, (7 irons work best) and an open space (a golf course, or a football field). You can't play regular golf but you can play lots of other games. For example, you could have a relay race in which teams line up with half the team on one end of the field, and the other half of the team on the other end of the field, about one hundred yards away (see diagram). The first person in line must hit the ball to the first person on the other half of his team as quickly as possible, and then that person returns it back to the original end of the field. Play continues until all the players have hit. The first team to complete this task wins. It's a lot of fun, and when you're in a hurry, a tennis ball hit by a golf club can go anywhere.

4. Whiffle Golf: Set up your own golf course just about anywhere you have room—an open field, all over a campground, around houses—usually with nine or eighteen holes. Each hole is a small tin can or jar just big enough for a "whiffle ball" to fit. The cans can be placed on the ground and anchored there, or they can be elevated on poles. After the course is set, each player gets a whiffle ball, and "tees-off" for hole number one. No clubs are used. You simply toss the ball underhanded except in a mixed group where the girls may toss overhanded. Each toss counts as a stroke. The idea is to get the ball into the can in the fewest strokes possible. It's best to play in foursomes as well to set a "par" for each hole, and print up scorecards. Schedule a Whiffle Golf tournament just like the pros. If you can't get whiffle balls, you can substitute bean-bags.

HAT AND GO SEEK

Here's a game that combines the best of "tag" and "hide-and-go-seek." One person wears an old hat, hides his eyes, and gives the rest of the group one minute to run and hide. Then, the hat-wearer begins to search. The hat must be worn, not carried.

When someone is found and tagged, that person must wear the hat, cover his eyes for twenty counts, and continue the search. Each person keeps a tally of how many times he wears the hat. The one who wears it the least number of times wins.

HORSEY BACK TAG

This game should be played on a grassy area. A horse and a rider are a team. The rider "mounts" the horse by jumping on the back of the horse with his arms around the horse's neck. The leader puts a piece of masking tape on each rider's back so that it is easily seen and reached. When the signal "mount up" is given, the riders mount their horses and attempt to round up the tape on the other riders' backs. The last rider left with tape on his back wins. Only the riders may take the tape off other riders. The horses are just horses, and if a horse falls, then the horse and rider are out of the game.

OVER THE LINE

Here's a softball game that has become very popular on Southern California beaches in recent years. All that is needed is a bat and a softball, six people (3 on a team), boundaries of the playing field that look like this:

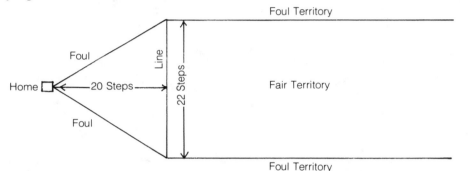

The batter on the team that is "up" stands at home plate and tries to hit the ball *over the line* in the air into fair territory. The ball is pitched from someone on the same team in one of two ways: (A) The "official" way is for the pitcher to kneel in front of the batter on the other side of the plate and toss the ball straight up for the batter to hit; (B) The pitch may also be delivered in the conventional manner with the pitcher standing fifteen or twenty feet from the batter and lobbing the ball up to be hit. The pitcher cannot interfere with the ball after it is hit, or the batter is out.

The team in the field positions themselves anywhere in fair territory. If they catch a hit ball before it hits the ground, the batter is out. Anything that drops into fair territory on the fly is a base hit. A ball hit in fair territory over the heads of all three fielders is a home run.

There are no bases, so there is no base running. When a person gets a base hit, the next batter comes up and hits. It takes three base hits before a run is scored, then every base hit after that adds another run. A home run after the first three base hits would score four runs, clearing the bases plus one bonus run, and it takes three more base hits to start scoring runs again. Here are some other rules:

1. Each batter has only two pitches and only one foul to get a hit. If you don't get a hit in two pitches, you're out.

2. Any ball hit on the ground in front of the line is an out, unless it's a foul on the first pitch.

3. Each team gets three outs per inning.

4. The game is played for nine innings.

The rules of the game can be modified. For example, the boundaries can be adjusted to fit the skills of the players, or instead of using a softball, you could use a mush ball or a volleyball, and you could vary team size. Be creative and have fun.

OVER THE LINE II

Here's a slightly more complicated version of the previous game. The playing field, the three person team, and the other rules remain much the same with a few modifications. For example, the field has two more lines, like so:

If the batter hits the ball between lines 1 and 2, it goes as a *single*. Between lines 2 and 3 is a double. Over line 3 is a *triple*, and over the head of the last opposing player is a *home run*. The defending players again can play anywhere in the field, but usually it is best to have one player defending each of the three territories.

The scoring is exactly like regular baseball but all runs must be forced home. For instance, if there's a man on first and second, and the next batter hits a double, then one run scores and now there are men on second and third. If the next guy hits a single, nobody scores since first base is open. Another single would score a run, since the bases are loaded.

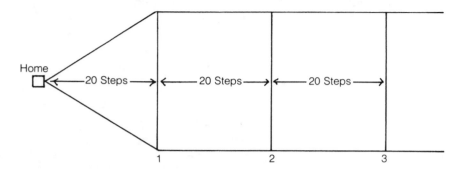

Singles, doubles, and triples are usually only counted as such when the ball crosses the appropriate line in the air. However, for more excitement and larger scores, play it this way: A single must land behind line 1 on the fly, but if the fielder lets it roll or bounce past line 2 in fair territory, then it's a double, even though it hit the ground in single territory. The same is true with a triple. If the ball crosses the third line, no matter how it got there, it goes as a triple. Home runs are still the same—over the head of everybody. All other rules are the same as regular Over the Line.

ROOFBALL

For this game, you need a volleyball and a roof. Experimentation will tell which roofs are the best. The unique thing about roofball is that each roof produces a new challenge, a different twist to the game. Decide on the out-of-bounds and form a single file line perpendicular to the line of the roof. The first in line serves the ball up on the roof and moves to the back of the line. Second in line must play the ball by hitting the ball volleyball-style back onto the roof before it hits the ground. He then moves to the back of the line, and the third player plays the ball. Action continues until a miss or a played ball lands out-of-bounds. Three missed balls and a player sits out. Last one in is the winner.

Missed balls are those that don't make it to the roof, hit under the roofline, go over the roof, are completely missed, are played while the player is in contact with the ground, or land out-of-bounds. The player who is responsible for the ball going out is charged with the miss. When you miss, you're out of the game, and the game continues until there is just one person left who is the winner. To play with teams, form two lines, one for each team. The first player on team one hits the ball up onto the roof, and the first player on team two hits it up again, then back to the second person on team one, and so on. Every time somebody misses, the other team gets points.

SHOE KICK

Have the kids remove one shoe and hang it from the end of their feet. The idea is to see who can "kick" his shoe the farthest. The kids will be surprised to see how many kick the shoes over their heads, behind them, or straight up in the air.

SARDINES

This game is actually "hide and seek" in reverse. The group chooses one person to be "it." This person hides, and the others try to find the hidden person. Each person should look individually, but small groups of two or three may look together. When a person find "it," he hides with "it" instead of telling the rest of the group. The hiding place may be changed an unlimited number of times during any game. The last person to find the hidden group, which now resembles a can of "sardines," is the loser or "it" for the next game.

SCAT

To play, you need a volleyball or playground ball. Everyone is assigned a number with two mystery numbers not assigned to anyone. The person who has the ball throws it up in the air and calls a number. Everyone scatters except the person whose number was called. He immediately retrieves the ball and yells "stop!" Then he tries to hit someone with the ball. If that person is hit, he gets letter S, C, A or T, and if the thrower misses, then he gets a letter. If a "mystery number," chosen by the leader, is called, then everyone gets a letter. People who get four letters, S-C-A-T, are eliminated.

SOCCER VARIATIONS

Soccer is an excellent game for small youth groups because you only need teams of five or six to play. You can play "official" soccer rules or try one of these soccer variations:

1. Crazy Soccer: This is regular soccer but with four teams and four goals. The teams can be of any size, but a minimum of two is best. The playing field should look something like this:

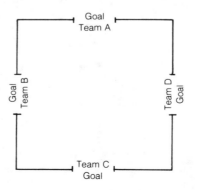

The size of the field can be determined by the number of players. Likewise, the size of the goals can vary, depending on the number and skill of the players. Goalies are optional. You can play with all four teams competing against each other at the same time; or, you can put two balls in play and have two games crisscrossing each other.

2. Croak Ball: This variation of soccer incorporates the use of old volleyball and croquet mallets turned sideways. The kids must push the ball with the mallets, not swing the mallets, to hit the ball. All other soccer rules apply.

3. Equal Rights Soccer: This is a good coed soccer game. Play regular soccer but have the guys tie their legs together with a piece of rope that is approximately two and a half feet long.

4. Monkey Soccer: Play this game with a light weight soccer ball. Regular soccer rules apply, except that the players must hit the ball with their fists. This means that players will have to bend their legs and swing their arms down low, like a monkey.

5. Line Soccer: Mark two parallel lines on the playing field about thirty feet apart. Each team lines up behind those two lines, facing each other, leaving the center area open. Team members may not stand more than ten feet behind their lines. Players should number off on each team. One number is called, and the two players with that number go to the center. The ball is thrown into the playing area, and the two players try to kick the ball across the other team's line past all the players. The players behind the lines try to stop the ball.

Players may try to kick the ball past the team line on the other side. But only the two players whose numbers are called can be in the middle area. After a goal is scored, two new numbers are called.

6. Silly Soccer: Play regular soccer but instead of using goals, set up several "pylons" that teams try to hit and knock over with the ball to score points. The object is to knock over all the other team's pylons.

7. Solo Soccer: This is the perfect soccer game for small groups in a limited area. Arrange the players in a circle. Mark a goal for each player by putting stakes in the ground about six or eight feet apart. You can also use pylons or chairs. The object is to protect your own goal while trying to score through someone else's. Each person is his own goalie. The last person to touch the ball before it passes through a goal receives one point. The person who is scored upon receives a negative point. Goals that are kicked above the head should not be allowed.

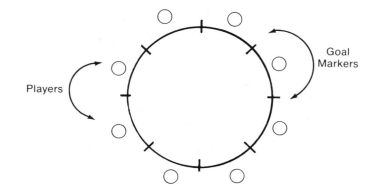

TAIL-GRAB

Divide the group into any number of equal "chains," lines of people where each person grips the wrist of the one in front of him. The last person in the chain has a handkerchief "tail" dangling behind. The object is for each front person to snatch the tail from another line. The fun is trying to maneuver to get someone else's tail while trying to keep your own.

TETHERBALL JUMP

Have eight to ten kids form a circle. Get in the center of the circle with a tether ball, a ball attached to a rope about eight feet long. Take the rope in your hand and begin making circles with the ball about six inches off the ground. The circle of kids move in closer, and each person must jump over the ball as it passes by. Keep going around and around, getting faster and faster and/or higher and higher, until someone goofs and is out. The last person in the game is the winner.

THREE BALL

Here's another variation of softball that can be used with almost any age group and any number of people. You need a baseball diamond and a combination of any three balls. Use softballs, footballs, rugby balls, soccer balls, volleyballs, or frisbees. You will also need a cardboard box, trash can, or bucket.

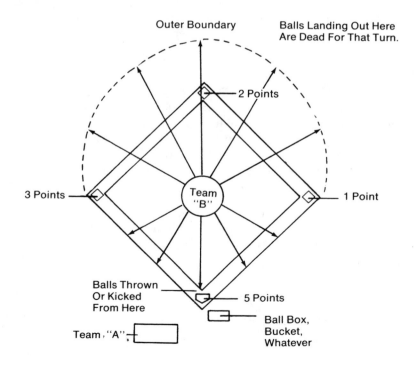

The box for the balls goes at home plate. One team is "up" and the other team is out in the field. There are no "positions." The first "batter" comes to the plate and selects three balls. He must get rid of all three balls as quickly as possible, anyway he wants—by kicking or throwing. The balls must stay within the boundaries of the field.

After getting rid of the balls, he starts running the bases while the team in the field tries to return all three balls back to the box at home plate. The player who is running the bases gets a point for each base he reaches before the balls are back in the box, and five points if he gets a "home run" and makes it all the way around. If a ball is caught on the fly, then that ball does not have to be placed in the box—it is dead. If the runner is caught between bases when the last of the three balls are placed in the box, then he loses all his accumulated points. He must watch and stop so that he is safely on a base when all the balls are finally in the box.

There are no "outs." The best way to play is let everyone on the team have a chance each inning and add up the total points scored. When everybody has batted, then the other team is "up." Play as many "innings" as desirable. If there are larger groups, then get several games going at once. It doesn't matter if the fields overlap.

Since it's very easy to get to first base, everyone can contribute to the team score and have fun. You will need one referee to blow the whistle when the balls come in and to help keep score. All the rules of this game can be adjusted, depending on the size and skill of the group.

THROUGH-THE-LEGS SHUFFLE

Here's the old "through-the-legs" game with a new twist. Have the teams line up single file behind the starting line, spreading their legs apart enough so that someone can crawl through them. Everyone must have his hands on the hips of the person in front of him. The last person crawls through the legs of the team and stands up at the front of the line. As soon as he stands up, the person who is now at the rear of the line crawls through. The lines move forward and the first team to cross the goal line wins. Only one person per team can be crawling at a time.

TUG-O-WAR

An old-fashioned tug-o-war never fails to be a winner. Get a thick, long rope and put one team on each end of it. Whichever team can pull the other one across the line or into a big mudhole is the winner.

VOLLEYBALL VARIATIONS

Volleyball is a stand-by for every youth group, but it can be improved and given new life by changing the rules in one of the following ways:

1. Badminton Volleyball: Get plenty of badminton racquets, and play a regular volleyball game using badminton racquets and a "birdie" rather than a volleyball.

2. Blind Volleyball: This is like regular volleyball, only the net should be a solid barrier so that neither team can see the other. Hang blankets all the way across the net. What makes this game fun is the element of surprise when the ball comes over the net.

3. Book Volleyball: This version of volleyball changes the game in two ways: First, everyone must use any size book instead of his hands to hit the ball. Second, a tennis ball or Nerf ball is used instead of a volleyball. Players should grip the book with both hands when hitting the ball.

4. Crazy Volleyball: It's just like regular volleyball, only each team may hit the ball four times before hitting it over the net. A ball hitting the floor counts as one hit; however, the ball may not hit the floor twice in succession. These rules keep the ball in play over a much longer period of time than in regular volleyball.

5. Elimination Volleyball: In this volleyball game, whoever makes a mistake or misses the ball goes out of the game. The teams keep getting smaller and smaller, and the team that manages to survive the longest is the winner.

6. Four Corner Volleyball: This variation of volleyball involves four teams at once. You can set it up with four volleyball nets or just two, depending on the size of your teams and the number of nets available. Arrange the nets according to one of the diagrams below. If you use two nets, then you form two right angles with them, as in Diagram A. If you use four nets, tie all four to the center pole as in Diagram B.

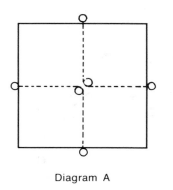

Diagram A

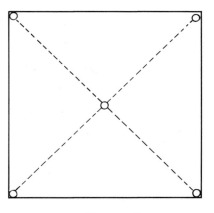

Diagram B

The four teams get in one of the four corners of the court, and the game is played like regular volleyball, except that now you can hit the ball to any of the other three teams. Interesting strategies develop since a team is never sure exactly when the ball will be coming its way.

7. Volley Volleyball: This game is like regular volleyball but with a new way to score points. The object is for a team to volley the ball as many times as possible up to fifty without missing or fouling before hitting it back over the net to the opposing team who will make every attempt to return it without missing. If they do miss, the opposite team receives as many points as they volleyed before sending it over the net. All volleys must be counted audibly by the entire team or by scorers on the sidelines. Other rules for this game are as follows:

1. No person may hit the ball two consecutive times.

2. No two people may hit the ball back and forth to each other more than once in succession to increase the number of volleys.

3. Five points are awarded to the serving team if the opposite team fails to return a serve.

4. Five points are awarded to the receiving team if a serve is missed, out-of-bounds, or in the net.

5. Players rotate on each serve, even if the serving team scores on successive serves.

6. A game is fifteen minutes. The highest score wins.

8. Water Volleyball: Place a pole in the middle of the volleyball net with a sprinkler to the top. Play a regular game of volleyball. This game would best be played on a dirt surface that will get muddy.

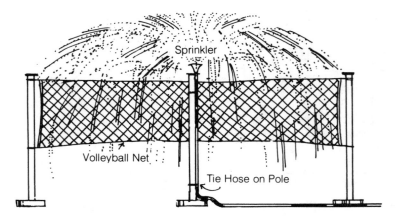

Sprinkler

Volleyball Net

Tie Hose on Pole

9. Volley Tennis: Volley Tennis is played on a tennis court with a volleyball. It's a great game for any number and requires little athletic ability. The serve is like regular volleyball, but the receiving team must let the ball *hit the court* before touching the ball. They are allowed three volleys to get the ball back across the net, but the ball must touch the court between each volley. The game ends at fifteen points, and only the serving team can score. Line hits are in play. This is most fun when at least a dozen people are on each team.

10. Water Balloon Volleyball: For this game, use water balloons instead of a volleyball. The serving team lobs a water balloon over the net, and someone on the other side must catch it without breaking it. He can then toss it back over, and the serving team must catch it. All tosses must be underhanded. No spikes are allowed. If the water balloon breaks on your side of the net, the other teams scores a point.

11. Volley Balloon Waterball: Same as above, only each team gets a sheet. The entire team surrounds the sheet, holding it by the edges. A water balloon is placed in the middle of the net. The other team must catch the balloon on the sheet without breaking it and heave it back over the net to the other team. This game takes teamwork.

WATER BALLOON SHOT PUT

This is a simple game to see who can toss a water balloon "shot put" style the farthest. To give the players added incentive, the youth leader can stand as a target just out of reach of the balloons.

WATER BALLOON TOSS

Have your kids pair off and stand opposite each other about two feet apart. Each couple gets a water balloon. At a signal, one person tosses the water balloon to his partner. The partner must catch it without breaking it. If he is successful, they each take one step backward. At the next signal, again the balloon is tossed. Each time one partner is successful, they move back another step. The couple that lasts the longest wins.

10

RELAY GAMES FOR SMALL YOUTH GROUPS

Relays are perfect for small youth groups because they can be used with any number of players and any number of teams. If you have exceptionally small teams (only two or three per team), you can make the game last longer by having each team member run the relay two or three times.

All relays are basically the same: Teams line up, and each team member must run the relay course or perform specific tasks in succession. The first team to have all its members complete the relay is the winner.

Here are some relay games for both indoors and outdoors and easily adaptable for your group's size.

BACK BALL RELAY

A ball, such as a basketball or volleyball, is placed between two players just above the belt line as the couple stands back-to-back. With their arms folded in front of them, they must carry the ball around a goal approximately thirty feet away.

BALLOON BAT RELAY

Teams line up single file with the kids as close together as possible. Each team gets a balloon. The person at the front of the line "bats" the balloon with his hand between his legs, and each successive team member does the same until it reaches the last person. That person runs it back to the front of the line, and the game continues until the team is back in its original order.

BALLOON POP RELAY

Each team member runs to a chair, blows up a balloon, and then sits on it to pop it.

BACK-TO-BACK RELAY

Couples must stand back-to-back and are tied together with a short rope. One person runs forward, and the other runs backward to the goal. On the return trip, the person who ran forward runs backward, and vice versa.

BALLOON SWEEP RELAY

Using a broom, players must sweep a balloon around a goal and back to the starting point.

BASKETBALL PASS

Teams line up single file. The player in front is given a basketball. The first player passes it to the player behind him *over his head*. The next person passes it *between his legs* to the person behind him, and so on. The last person in line gets the ball, goes to the front of the line, and starts the whole process over again. The first team to get back in its original order wins.

BASKETBALL SQUAT

Divide into teams, and choose captains. Have the teams line up in a straight line facing the captains and approximately five to ten feet away from them. The captain throws the ball to the first person in the line who returns the throw and then squats down. The captain then throws the ball to the second person who does the same. The captain then throws the ball a second time to the last person who throws it back and stands back up. This pattern is repeated till everyone has received another pass. Anytime the ball is dropped, the team must start over again. The first team to get everybody standing up again is the winner.

BAT ROUND RELAY

Place a baseball bat for each team at one end of the playing area with the team lined up at the other end. Each player runs to the bat, puts his forehead on the bat in a vertical position and then runs around the bat ten times while still in that position. Then he must return to his team without falling down.

BLINDMAN CHARIOT RACES

Girls ride on the shoulders of guys while the guys are blindfolded. They shout directions to the guys as they run around an obstacle course.

BOTTLE FILL RELAY

Each team appoints one kid to lie on the floor at a certain distance with an bottle on his forehead. Each team member runs to that person with a nonbendable cup filled with water and tries to fill the bottle. The bottle should be large enough that it takes quite a few cups full of water to fill it. The first team to fill their bottle wins.

BROOM JUMP RELAY

Team members should stand two abreast. The first couple on each team is given a broom. On "go," each one grabs one end of the broom, and they run back through their team, holding the broom just above the floor. Everyone must jump over the broom. When the couple reaches the back of the line, they must pass the broom back to the front of the line, using hands only. Then each couple repeats the relay. The first team with the original couple again heading the team wins.

The People Who Brought You This Book...

invite you to discover MORE valuable youth ministry resources.

Youth Specialties offers an assortment of books, publications, tapes and events, all designed to encourage and train youth workers and their kids. Just return this card, and we'll send you FREE information on our products and services.

Please send me the FREE Youth Specialties Catalog and information on upcoming Youth Specialties events.

Name_____

Church/Org._____

Address_____

City_____State_____Zip_____

Phone Number ( )_____

The People Who Brought You This Book...

invite you to discover MORE valuable youth ministry resources.

Youth Specialties offers an assortment of books, publications, tapes and events, all designed to encourage and train youth workers and their kids. Just return this card, and we'll send you FREE information on our products and services.

Please send me the FREE Youth Specialties Catalog and information on upcoming Youth Specialties events.

Name_____

Church/Org._____

Address_____

City_____State_____Zip_____

Phone Number ( )_____

Call toll-free to order:
(800) 776-8008

BUSINESS REPLY MAIL
FIRST CLASS   PERMIT NO. 16   EL CAJON, CA

POSTAGE WILL BE PAID BY ADDRESSEE

YOUTH SPECIALTIES
1224 Greenfield Dr.
El Cajon, CA 92021-9989

Il·l···I·Ill····I·l···Ill·l·I·l·I·l·l·I····Ill

Call toll-free to order:
(800) 776-8008

NO POSTAGE
NECESSARY
IF MAILED
IN THE
UNITED STATES

BUSINESS REPLY MAIL
FIRST CLASS   PERMIT NO. 16   EL CAJON, CA

POSTAGE WILL BE PAID BY ADDRESSEE

YOUTH SPECIALTIES
1224 Greenfield Dr.
El Cajon, CA 92021-9989

Il·l···I·Ill····I·l···Ill·l·I·l·I·l·l·I····Ill

BROOM TWIST RELAY

At a point twenty or thirty feet away, a team leader stands, holding a broom. When the game begins, each player runs to his team leader, takes the broom, holds it against his chest with the bristles over his head. Looking up at the broom, the player must turn around as fast as possible ten times, while the leader counts the number of turns. Then the player hands the broom back to the leader, dizzily runs back to the team and tags the next player.

CATERPILLAR RELAY

This is a good game for camps. Have the kids bring their sleeping bags and do races in them. Line the teams up, relay style. The first person in line gets in the sleeping bag head first and races to a certain point and back, listening to the shouted directions from his team. The first team finished is the winner. As a variation, have the kids crawl in their sleeping bags like a caterpillar.

COIN, BOOK, AND BALL RELAY

Each team is given one quarter, one tennis ball, and a book. Balance the book on your head, hold the quarter in your eye, place the ball between your knees, then walk to the finish line. No hands are to be used.

COTTON BALL RACE

Provide each team with a number of cotton balls in a container, such as a dish or a pan, a spatula and an egg carton.

At a signal, the first person picks up a cotton ball with the spatula and keeps it balanced on the spatula while running to a goal and back. If he loses the cotton ball, he must start over. When he returns to his team, he places the cotton ball in the egg carton. The first team to fill their egg carton wins.

EGG AND SPOON RELAY

Give each player a spoon. The teams line up, and a dozen eggs are placed at one end of the line. The players must pass the eggs down the line using the spoons only. The winning team gets the most unbroken eggs down the line in the fastest time.

EGG ROLL

Contestants roll a raw egg along an obstacle course with their noses. If the egg breaks, the player must start over with a new egg.

FEATHER RELAY

Give each team a box of small feathers, one per team member. Mallard or duck breast feathers are best. At a signal, the first person blows his feather the length of the room and into a small box without touching the feather. He may blow an opponent's feather in the opposite direction. The race continues until all the feathers are in the box. This race can be doubly exciting if done on hands and knees.

FOREHEAD RACE

Each couple races to a point and back carrying a grapefruit or balloon between their foreheads. If it is dropped, they must start over.

FRISBEE RELAY

This is a good outdoor relay. Divide the group into equally sized teams of five or six. Any number of teams can play at once. Each team will need a frisbee. Each team should spread out in a line about fifty feet or more apart. The first person throws the frisbee to the second person, who allows the frisbee to land, goes where it landed, and then throws it towards the third person. The object is to see which team can throw it the greatest distance in the shortest time. Award points for throwing it the farthest and for finishing first.

GOTCHA RELAY

Divide the group into two teams. Set up the area similar to the diagram below. Each team lines up single file behind their respective markers. On "go," the first players begin running around the track in one direction only. On completing the lap, the runner tags the next player.

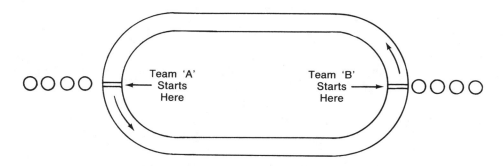

The object of the game is to tag the runner of the other team. The teams continue to run laps until a person is finally Gotcha. The team that catches the other first is the winner. Be sure to divide the teams so that they are about even in speed.

GRAB BAG RELAY

Teams line up single file behind a line. A paper bag containing individually wrapped edible items is placed on a chair at the opposite end of the room. At a signal, the first person runs to the chair, sits down, reaches into the bag without looking, pulls out an item, unwraps it, and eats it. When he has swallowed the entire package contents, the "official" okays it, and he runs back to the starting position, and the next contestant takes his turn. Each contestant *must* eat whatever he grabs out of the bag. The first team to finish the contents of the grab bag wins. Suggestions for grab bag: pickles, olives, cereal, onions, candy, and carrots.

GUZZLE RELAY

Give each person a drinking straw. A gallon of apple cider is placed a certain distance away. When you blow the whistle, the first person in line runs to the cider and starts guzzling through the straw. When the whistle blows again, he stops and the next person drinks. Some people get a short drink; others a long drink. The team that finishes their gallon of cider first is the winner.

HAND-IN-GLOVE RELAY

Teams stand in line and pass a pair of gloves from one end to the other. Each person takes the gloves off the person in front of him and puts them on himself. All fingers of the hand must fit in the fingers of the gloves. Use rubber kitchen gloves or large work gloves.

HANDS FULL RELAY

Assemble two identical sets of at least twelve miscellaneous items (i.e., 2 brooms, 2 balls, 2 skillets, 2 rolls of bathroom tissue, 2 ladders). Place the two sets of objects on two separate tables.

Line up a team for each table. The first player for each team runs to this table, picks up one item, and takes it back to the second player. Once picked up, an item cannot touch the table or floor. The second player and each succeeding player carries the items collected by his teammates to the table, picks up one new item, and carries them all back to the next player. The game will begin rapidly, but the pace will slow as each player decides which item to add to a growing armload of items. It will also take increasingly longer for one player to pass his burden to the next player in line.

Any item that is dropped in transit or transfer must be returned to the table by the leader. No one may assist the giving and receiving player in the exchange of items except through coaching. The first team to empty the table wins.

INNER TUBE RELAY

Each team chooses couples and lines up in different areas of the room. Two inner tubes are placed in the center of the room. Starting with the tube over their heads, each couple must run to the inner tube and squeeze through it together. The first team to have all the couples finish wins.

LEMON RELAY

Teams line up in straight lines. The first person is given a pencil and a lemon and asked to push the lemon to the finish line and back using only the pencil. If the lemon goes out of the lane, start over.

LIFESAVER RELAY

Give each player a toothpick to hold in his teeth. Place a lifesaver on the toothpick of the players at the head of each line. It is then passed from toothpick to toothpick until it reaches the end of the line. If it's dropped before it reaches the end of the line, it must be started over again at the beginning of the line. The winning team is the one whose lifesaver reaches the end of the line first.

MAD RELAY

In this relay race, each contestant does something different. At a signal, the first person on each team runs to a chair where there is bag containing instructions written on separate pieces of paper. The contestant draws one of the instructions, reads it, and follows it as quickly as

157

possible. Before returning to the team, the contestant must tag the chair. The contestant then runs back and tags the next runner. The team that uses all of its instructions first is the winner. Here are a few samples:

1. Run around the chair five times while continuously yelling "The British are coming, the British are coming."

2. Run to the nearest person on another team and scratch his head.

3. Run to the nearest adult in the room and whisper "You're no spring chicken."

4. Stand on one foot while holding the other in your hand, tilt your head back, and count "10, 9, 8, 7, 6, 5, 4, 3, 2, 1, Blast off!"

5. Take your shoes off, put them on the wrong feet, and then tag your nearest opponent.

6. Sit on the floor, cross your legs, and sing the following: "Mary had a little lamb, little lamb, little lamb, Mary had a little lamb, its fleece was white as snow."

7. Go to the last person on your team and make three different "funny-face" expressions.

8. Put your hands over your eyes and snort like a pig five times and meow like a cat five times.

9. Sit in the chair, fold your arms, and laugh hard and loud for five seconds.

10. Run around the chair backwards five times while clapping your hands.

11. Go to a blonde and keep asking "Do blondes really have more fun?" until he answers.

12. Run to someone not on your team, kiss his hand, and gently pinch his cheek.

MESSAGE RELAY

Divide each team in half and stand the two halves in parallel lines a distance (at least ten feet, preferably more) from each other. Write a crazy message on a piece of paper (sample: "Mrs. Sarah Sahara tells extraordinary information to very enterprising executives."). Give a copy to the first member of each team, who reads it, wads it up, throws it on the ground, and runs across the distance to the first person on his team in the *opposite* line, and whispers the message in his ear. That person then runs to the next team member in the opposite line and whispers the message to him—and so on until the last person on the team hears the message and runs to the game leader to whisper the message to him. The team closest to the original message wins. Accuracy, not time, is most important—but they must run.

PAPER CHASE

Each person is given two pieces of paper and must travel between two points stepping only on the paper.

PING-PONG RELAY

Select several kids to race ping-pong balls. Each player gets a party blower that uncoils when blown. He pushes the balls across the floor using only those blowers. First across the finish line wins.

POTATO RELAY

Teams line up. Each player must push the potato along the floor to a goal and back using only his nose.

ROLLERSKATE RELAY

Get a couple pair of skates, preferably the kind that clamp onto your street shoes. Give each team a pair of skates. Each team member must put on the skates and skate around a goal and return.

SACK RACE

Get some old burlap bags and have kids race with their feet inside them, hopping to the goal and back.

SKI RELAY

Construct "skis" out of plywood and nail old shoes to them. Divide your group into teams. Each member of the team must put on the "skis," ski to a pole, go around it, and return.

SOCK TAIL RELAY

Make several "sock tails" and give one to each team. A sock tail consists of a belt with a sock tied onto it and an orange in the end of the sock as a weight. The first person on each team puts on the tail with the sock hanging down from his rear. Another orange is placed on the floor. At the signal, the player must push the orange on the floor to a goal and back with the sock tail. If he touches the orange with his feet or hands, he must start over.

SPOON RELAY

Each player holds a plastic spoon in his mouth. The leader places a marble in the spoon of each of the players at the head of the line and it is passed from spoon to spoon until it reaches the end of the line. The team that gets their marble to the end of the line first is the winner.

SUCKER RELAY

Each person has a paper straw. A piece of paper about 4 inches square is picked up by sucking on the straw and is carried around a goal and back. If you drop the paper, you must start over.

THIMBLE RELAY

Teams form a line, and each player has a straw that he holds upright in his mouth. The relay is started by placing the thimble on the straw held by the first person in line and passed from player to player. The team that gets the thimble to the end of the line first is the winner.

THREE-LEGGED RACE

Here's another favorite. Two players from each team stand side by side and their legs nearest each other are tied together. They then race to the goal and back.

TYPHOON

This game is ideal for the summer. Have two lines, single file, facing a water source. At a signal, the first person in each line runs down to the water, fills a bucket, runs back to his team, and throws the water in the face of his teammate. Before the person can throw the water, his teammate must point and yell "Typhoon." Each person takes the bucket down to the water and returns to storm his team. The first line to finish is declared the winner. For safety reasons, the participants should be a least three feet from those receiving the water, and a plastic bucket should be used.

WADDLE RELAY

In this relay, teams race with players carrying a small coin between their knees. They must successfully drop the coin into a milk bottle or jar placed fifteen or twenty feet away without using their hands. If the coin is dropped along the way, the player must start over.

WAGON RELAY

For this game, you will need to obtain one or more kids' wagons. Each team pairs off. One person sits in the wagon and uses the handle to steer while the other person pushes him or her around a slalom course. When one couple finishes, the next begins, and the first team to have everyone complete the course wins.

A variation is to have one person just sitting in the wagon while the other steers and pushs the wagon backward through the course.

WEIRDBARROW RELAY

This is a variation of a wheelbarrow race where player A becomes the wheelbarrow by walking on his hands while player B uses player A's feet as handles and runs along behind. In this relay the added difficulty is that the wheelbarrow (player A) must push a volleyball along the ground with his nose.

WILD WHEELBARROW RELAY

This relay requires one or more real wheelbarrows. Team members pair off, with one person pushing the wheelbarrow and the other riding in the wheelbarrow. They must travel around a goal and back; however, the wheelbarrow driver is blindfolded and the person sitting in the wheelbarrow must give him directions.

11

SPECIAL EVENTS AND SOCIAL ACTIVITIES FOR SMALL YOUTH GROUPS

Special events are activities that are normally planned for weekend nights, holidays, and other special occasions for fun and fellowship. They are very important for a small youth group as community-builders, as a way to attract young people who might not ordinarily attend more "serious" youth group functions, and as a positive way to have fun. Special events are also excellent opportunities for cooperation with other youth groups.

Most small youth groups find it sufficient to plan approximately one special event each month and vary their annual youth group calendar with different activities. For example, have a scavenger hunt one month, an overnight retreat the next, and a trip to an amusement park the next. There will be favorite special events that your young people will want to repeat on a regular or annual basis, but encourage creativity and originality when planning them.

Be sure to promote your special events enthusiastically. Announce them several weeks in advance, put up a few posters, send out a mailing, and make certain your kids phone everyone.

At the event itself, provide enough adult sponsors and chaperones to satisfy parents and insure the success of the activity. Take slides or video movies of the activities and show them later to the group at a regular youth group meeting. Photos may be used to add to or start your youth group scrapbook or newsletter.

The ideas presented in this chapter are deliberately brief and intended to spark your own creativity. Brainstorm further ideas with your youth and with your adult leaders. Most of these and other ideas are described in much greater detail in the Youth Specialties *Ideas* books.

SCAVENGER HUNTS

A scavenger hunt is always fun for a small youth group. The concept is simple: You give kids a list of items, and they go out and bring back as many items on the list as they possibly can within the time limit. Kids can "hunt" in small groups of two or three or they can hunt in larger teams, depending on the number of kids. After the hunt is over, you can have a party, award prizes to the winners, play some other games, and serve refreshments.

You can make any scavenger hunt "new" by changing its theme or doing it in a new way. Here are a few great scavenger hunt ideas:

1. Polaroid Scavenger Hunt: Divide into two teams and give each team an instant camera, a couple rolls of film, and a list of pictures that they have to take, develop, and bring back. Pictures can be worth more or less points depending on their difficulty. Pictures can include things like "your group up in a tree," "your group in the backseat of a police car," or "your group doing a pyramid in the Fair Oaks Shopping Mall."

2. Sound Scavenger Hunt: This is like the Polaroid Scavenger Hunt, except that you give each team a cassette tape recorder, a blank tape, and a list of "sounds" that they must record and bring back. Sounds can include "a dog barking," "a police siren," "a cuckoo clock," or "someone over sixty-five explaining what the term 'heavy metal' means."

3. Scripture Scavenger Hunt: Kids must bring back items that can be found in the Bible and produce a Bible verse that specifically mentions it.

4. Crazy Creative Scavenger Hunt: Give each scavenger team a list of items that do not make sense, such as a "dip flipper," a "giant wahoo," a "yellow grot grabber," a "snail egg," or a "portable electric thumb twiddly dummer." The kids must bring back items that they think fit the descriptive names. A team of judges can then determine which team actually brought back the "real" item.

5. Action Scavenger Hunt: Give each team a list of things they must *do* , like "Sing a verse of Amazing Grace," "Run around the house twice," "Get a guided tour of the kitchen," or "Sweep up the garage." Kids go to various homes and perform these tasks, asking the people at each house to sign their sheet to verify that they actually did it. Only one item per house allowed.

6. The Great Race: Give each team a list of questions that they must answer at various locations, such as "Who made the light pole on the corner of Main and Broadway?"; "How many light bulbs are burnt out on the Pizza Parlor sign at Fifth and Mapleview?"; "How many red lights are flashing on the KSON radio tower?" They must return with as many correct answers as possible. This game can also be played in a shopping mall and named "The Great Shopping Mall Derby."

7. Pizza Scavenger Hunt: Kids try to collect pizza ingredients on their scavenger hunt. When they return, they have a pizza party.

8. Service Scavenger Hunt: This scavenger hunt takes the emphasis from "getting" to "giving." Give each team a list of items: "Mow someone's lawn," "Clean all the windows on the front of someone's house," "Empty all the wastebaskets in someone's home," or "Wash someone's car." Make sure the kids do a good job at each location.

9. People Scavenger Hunt: Some groups have called this a "Manhunt." Give each group a list of people to either bring back with them or just autograph their sheet. Examples: "someone over six feet tall," "someone with braces on their teeth," "someone who can play a banjo," "someone on the football team," or "someone who has a twin brother or sister."

OUT ON THE TOWN

There are many things your group can do together just for fun around town. Here are some sample ideas:

1. Go to a movie together: Pick a good one and then discuss it later.

2. Go to a concert together: This can be a Christian music concert or a secular concert.

3. Video Game Night: Depending on the size of your group, you might be able to rent a local video arcade for a nominal price or get a group price for tokens.

4. Go to an amusement park: If you have tourist attractions in your area, go together as a youth group. Theme parks, zoos, historical sites, and museums make excellent outings for a small youth group.

5. Go shopping: This is an especially good idea around Christmas time. Pick a day or evening when your group can go Christmas shopping together in a shopping mall.

HAVE A PARTY

Every youth group enjoys a party! Here are a few ideas:

1. Theme Parties: You can create a successful party around almost any theme. The most common are holiday themes—a Christmas party, a Halloween party, a Valentine's Day Party, a Grad Night party. But there are countless other themes to help build a party. For example, use a "banana" theme and call it a "Banana Night." Kids wear banana colors (yellow, green, or brown), play banana games ("bob" for bananas), eat banana splits, and literally "go bananas." How about an "Orange Night," a "Punk Party," or a "Fifties Night?" Decide on a theme, then brainstorm some good games and activities to fit the theme.

2. Beach or Swim Parties: If you have access to a pool or if you live near the beach, a swim party will always be popular with kids during the summer. Organize some pool or beach games as well (see the Youth Specialties *Ideas* books for some good suggestions).

3. A Hawaiian Luau: Schedule this activity in midwinter. Have everyone wear shorts, sandals, and other beach wear. Decorate with travel posters, palm trees, and sun lamps. Show a surfing movie, have a hula contest, and serve a Polynesian dinner.

4. Christmas Masquerade Party: Have all the kids wear a Christmas costume to the party. See the book, *Holiday Ideas for Youth Groups,* by Rice and Yaconelli (Zondervan Publishing House) for other good Christmas party activities.

5. A Food Party: Any party that involves food will be a success with young people. Have a

165

"Burger Bash," a "Pizza Party," or an "Ice Cream Social." You might want to try an "Awful Waffle Party," make waffles and put all kinds of toppings on them.

6. Movie Night: Show home movies or rent some video movies. Serve popcorn and soft drinks.

7. Once a Year Birthday Party: Celebrate everyone's birthday all at once. Have a big birthday cake, play typical birthday party games, and sing "Happy Birthday" to each person.

PROGRESSIVE DINNERS

Another favorite social is the progressive dinner. Normally, it's done by transporting the group from one place to another with a different "course" of the meal served at each location (appetizer, soup, salad, main course, dessert). But you might want to try one of these creative variations:

1. Backwards Progressive Dinner: The meal is served in reverse order, but so is everything else. People should wear their clothes inside out, walk backward, and so on. Use your imagination.

2. Bike Progressive Dinner: Progress from house to house on bikes or try some other mode of transportation, like roller skates, or jogging.

3. International Progressive Dinner: Each course of the meal should be food from a different country, e.g., Mexican, Chinese, German, Italian, and French.

4. Dessert Progressive Dinner: Feature different desserts at each location.

5. Junk Food Progressive Dinner: Travel from one fast-food restaurant to another, beginning with an appetizer (french fries), salad, drink, main course (hamburger), and dessert.

6. Treasure Hunt Progressive Dinner: Kids must solve clues to discover the location of the next course of the meal. This adds a little excitement and competition to the event.

RECREATIONAL ACTIVITIES

Here are some ideas for special events that involve games and recreation:

1. Skating Party: Go to a local skating rink or have all the kids bring their skates to the church and use the church parking lot for a variety of games on skates.

2. Miniature Golf: Most cities and towns have one or more "putt-putt" golf courses that offer challenging and interesting golf games. Some also offer batting cages, video games, and other activities.

3. Tournament: Your youth group can sponsor a volleyball tournament, a racquetball tournament, a tennis tournament, or a bowling tournament. Invite other groups.

4. Square Dance: A square dance is a lot of fun for youth groups. Many kids may think of it as "hokey," but if you can get a good "caller" and promote it with enthusiasm, your kids will be surprised at how much fun it can be.

5. Game Day: Have a day or an evening of games, one after another, like those provided in this book. Call it "Super Saturday" or a "R.I.O.T." (Ridiculous, Incredible, Outstanding, and Terrific!)

6. Bike Events: Have a bike hike or a bike "rodeo."

7. Ski Trips: Snow skiing or water skiing.

8. Jogathon: Many kids enjoy running for fitness and fun.

TREASURE HUNTS AND OTHER CAR RALLIES

Like scavenger hunts, treasure hunts have been popular with youth groups for a long time. The group is divided into teams; each team tries to be the first to reach the "treasure" by solving a series of clues. Ordinarily, the first clue is given to each group at the starting point and leads them to the first of several locations. At each subsequent location, the group receives an additional clue until they finally reach the treasure.

There are two ways to make a treasure hunt completely new: (1) Find some unusual clues, and (2) find some unusual treasures. Here are a few ideas for some creative treasure hunts and car rallies:

1. Wild Goose Chase: The "treasure" is a live goose. You can substitute other animals and name your hunt accordingly. For more exotic animals, you may want to use a reasonable facsimile.

2. Holiday Hunts: Treasure hunts work well with holiday themes. Have a "Witch Hunt" or a "Great Pumpkin Hunt" at Halloween, or a "Giant Easter Hunt" at Easter.

3. Scripture Treasure Hunt: All the clues in this treasure hunt are verses from the Bible. Using a concordance, you can find verses that contain words or phrases identifying possible locations.

4. Caroling Treasure Hunt: At Christmas, divide into small "caroling groups." At each location, have the group sing a few carols before they get the next clue. Locations can include nursing homes and other places where caroling would be welcome.

5. Bigger and Better Hunt: To begin this event, give each group a penny. They must then go to someone's home and see what they can buy at that house for one penny. Whatever they get, they take somewhere else and try to trade it for something else, preferably something of greater value. They continue trading until the end of the time limit. The winning team is the team that comes back with the item of the greatest value. These items can then be donated to charity.

6. Wanderlust: Teams travel in cars or on bikes. Each team gets one dice, which they roll at each intersection. If they roll a "1" or "2," they go left. If they roll a "3" or "4," they go right. If they roll a "5" or "6," they go straight ahead. At the end of the time limit, the team that has traveled the farthest is the winner.

7. Hot or Cold Car Rally: Each team travels in a car with a youth sponsor or volunteer adult driver. The kids are blindfolded. The driver is the only one who knows where the "treasure" or the final destination is. At each intersection, the kids are asked whether they want to go right, left, or straight ahead. The driver does whatever the group says. Every sixty seconds the driver tells the group whether they are getting "hot" or "cold." It's best for the kids to decide which way they want to go *before* they get to the intersection so that the driver may safely get into the proper lanes.

FAMILY EVENTS

Plan a few events each year with your youth group that include families or parents. Here are some examples:

1. A Family Picnic: Organize a picnic for each family in the youth group and ask the young people to plan all the games and activities.

2. Mother's-Father's Day Banquet: Figure out which day falls exactly halfway between Mother's and Father's Day. This is the perfect time for a "Mother's-Father's Day Banquet." Have the kids prepare the meal and put on a program to honor all the parents who attend.

3. Parents' Night Out: Plan a party for all the little brothers and sisters so that an evening is left free for the parents to go out alone.

4. Parents' Party: Plan a party and invite all the parents. There are many games that can be played with parents, like charades, relays, and sports. You might want to have a parents vs. kids volleyball game.

RETREATS AND EASY OVERNIGHTERS

There are all kinds of overnight events that are easy to do with a small youth group. Here are a few examples:

1. Lock-in: This is essentially a "slumber party" held at the church. Have the kids bring their sleeping bags to camp out inside the church building. Play games, show movies, have plenty of snacks, and the kids will love it.

2. Tent Retreat: Find a local campground and borrow or rent enough tents for your group. It's a great way to do a weekend retreat without the normal expense of securing a retreat center.

3. Back Packs: Most national forests only allow groups of twelve or fifteen into the back country areas anyway, so a back pack makes an excellent overnight trip for a small youth group. In most cities, there are places where you can rent all the gear you need. It's a great experience for kids.

4. Motel Retreats: A small youth group can have an outstanding retreat using a small motel that has a swimming pool, meeting room, and restaurant. Many smaller motels offer rooms at very reasonable rates.

SPY VS. SPY

Here's one final idea that has proven to be very successful with small youth groups. It requires cooperation with a youth group from another church and advance preparation.

First, you must take a photo of your entire youth group or get individual photos of each person in the group. These photos are then sent to the other youth group a week or so before the event takes place.

At a scheduled day or time, the two youth groups go to a busy place, like a shopping mall or an airport. Each group should meet at a predetermined place, but one group should not know where the other one is. Then at a set time, the two groups disperse and try to locate each other, working individually or in pairs. The kids try to find members of the other youth group by remembering them from the photos. Whenever someone thinks he has located someone from the other group, he goes to that person and says "You're under arrest!" Whoever says this key phrase first gets points for his group. If a person is "arrested" three times, he must go to "jail" (some predetermined place) and stay there for the rest of the game. The game can last thirty minutes to an hour.

If you provide names with the photos, a person can get extra points by saying "You're under arrest, Jennifer!" Have a party afterward with refreshments. It's a good way to get to know another youth group.

12

SERVICE PROJECTS FOR SMALL YOUTH GROUPS

Inevitably small youth groups feel lifeless sometimes due to their smallness. One of the best ways to revitalize a struggling, lethargic youth group is to challenge the young people to be involved in ministry and service to others.

Jon Johnston, in his book *Will Evangelicalism Survive Its Popularity* (Zondervan) tells an interesting story about a man who was caught in an Alaskan blizzard. The man wandered aimlessly, preparing himself for inevitable death. Most parts of his body were numb, so he decided to give up without resistance. Just before slumping over into a snowbank, he heard a faint whimper. At his feet lay a small puppy, who faced the same predicament as he. Forgetting his own misery, he picked up the dog and vigorously rubbed his fur. The dog revived, and the man also felt warmer. By helping the dog, he was able to last through the night. Likewise, Johnston points out, when we make a conscious and determined effort to serve others in Christ's name, we insure our own survival as well. This is especially true with small youth groups.

No youth group is too small to do great things for God. All God needs is the availability of your young people and their willingness to be used. Even the smallest deeds of kindness and mercy bring everlasting dividends. As the hymn writer penned "Little is much when God is in it." Mission and service is the best way for a small youth group to feel full of life.

The following ideas are reprinted with permission from the book *Ideas for Social Action* by Anthony Campolo (Youth Specialties/Zondervan). Here are a few:

ADOPT A GRANDPARENT

This service project is for young people who are mature enough to make a long-term commitment. The first step is to take the entire group to visit a convalescent (nursing) home. Allow the kids to mingle and talk with these people so that they get to know them better.

Afterward, introduce them to the idea of "adopting" one or more of these seniors as a "grandparent(s)." Each young person would be assigned or would choose one or two elderly people to visit on a regular basis, to remember on special occasions, to take on short trips, and to be a good friend. This could be planned to continue for a specific amount of time, perhaps a year or maybe even longer.

During the course of the project, the young people can share with each other how things are going and what problems they are encountering. The adult youth sponsors need to monitor the project and offer help and encouragement to the kids who are involved. Either at the end of the project or at the end of the year, the group can sponsor a special banquet. Most young people will find this project very rewarding, and the elderly people will appreciate it greatly.

CONVALESCENT HOME MINISTRY

There are hundreds of thousands of elderly people who reside in convalescent hospitals (nursing homes) all over the country. In most cases, they are there because they need regular medical or nursing care. These resident hospitals provide youth groups with a tremendous opportunity for service. It is likely that there are several convalescent homes close to your church or community that would love to have your group involved in voluntary service.

Every convalescent home has an "activities director" who will gladly give you information and help you plan whatever you choose to do. It is important for you to begin by contacting either this person or the administrator of the convalescent home to find out whether the services of your group will be welcomed. Most convalescent homes have a difficult time finding people to come and do things for their patients, and the patients especially enjoy young people. The activities director will probably be available to present an "orientation" program for the youth group.

Even though convalescent homes take care of people who are losing many of their physical abilities, they are basically normal human beings. They are often very old but otherwise they are just like everyone else. They enjoy being around people; they respond to a smile, a touch, kind words, music, and laughter. Your youth group can provide these things for men and women who often feel isolated from the outside world. Here is a list of other possibilities:

1. Begin some one-on-one visits, perhaps as part of an "Adopt a Grandparent" program. These visits can include conversation, reading to them, writing letters for them, or just being a good listener.

2. Take them on some short trips. Most residents of convalescent homes are permitted to leave the hospital for field trips, such as a going to a restaurant, a movie, a high school football game, or church. This can be arranged with the hospital, and the patients love it. Some convalescent homes will plan their own outings for the patients, like going to the zoo or a shopping center, your group can help push the wheelchairs. Sometimes all that is needed is someone to push them around the block or even around the parking lot.

3. Call the elderly on the phone. Most residents of convalescent homes enjoy talking to someone who is interested in them. Once your kids have established a relationship in person, a regular phone-calling program can work both ways—with the kids calling the residents, and the residents knowing that they are free to call their young friends anytime.

4. Bring programs to the convalescent home, such as special music, plays, and skits. Use the meeting hall at a local nursing home for your regular youth group meeting and allow the patients to participate. Or provide a regular Bible Study for the convalescent home—schedule all events with the activities director.

5. Provide music for the patients. If you have any young people who are talented in music, encourage them to share their music with the elderly, especially old hymns and old songs.

6. Play games with convalescent home residents. Most of the patients can play games such as Scrabble, Checkers, or Dominoes. There are even some inactive group games that can be played with them.

7. Provide gifts for the elderly. Like most people, they enjoy receiving gifts of love now and then. For example, a baseball cap to protect their heads when they go outside, a pouch that they can hang on the side of their wheelchair to keep things in, a small bouquet of flowers, a book, or tape for them to enjoy can be very appropriate. They also enjoy giving gifts, and they will.

8. Bring pets or small children to the convalescent home. Most of the residents have almost forgotten what it feels like to hold a small puppy or a kitten, or to touch a small child. Something as ordinary as that can be a great source of joy for an elderly person who is confined to a nursing home.

9. Plant a garden for the patients. There will usually be a small plot of ground near the convalescent home where you can prepare the soil and plant a garden. Let the patients choose what they would like to plant. Let them help take of it. Some people will look forward each day to going out and watering their tomato plants and watching them grow.

There's really no limit to the things that you can do in a convalescent home. Think creatively and take advantage of this crucial ministry that is right at home. If you aren't aware of any convalescent homes in your area, check the yellow pages of your telephone directory, your local doctor, or contact the American Health Care Association (1200 Fifteenth Street, N.W., Washington D.C., 20005) for a listing of local and state nursing home associations.

LETTERS TO THE EDITOR

On crucial political issues, write letters to the editor of your local newspaper. These are usually published and read by hundreds, sometimes thousands of people including candidates and policymakers. Here you will have a significant forum for expressing your political views from a Christian perspective. Don't sign the letter in such a way that it looks like it comes from your entire group or church; this isn't honest or fair to those who may not share your views.

LETTER-WRITING CAMPAIGNS

Never underestimate the importance of organizing a letter-writing campaign on an important social-political issue. Congressmen and candidates are very much influenced by the flow of mail. The letters should all address themselves to the issue and state whether they are for or against a particular piece of legislation, but each person should write the letter in his own words and style.

Bread for the World is one organization that attempts to keep Christian people aware of important legislation affecting the poor and needy of the world. It encourages churches to send an "Offering of Letters" to local members of congress to influence them in the right direction. Even though in some cases the volume of mail may be too great to read, a careful record is always kept of letters "for" or "against" every issue. Voting is done on the basis of that record.

MINISTRY TO THE RETARDED

In every city there are institutions that care for people who are "developmentally handicapped" or mentally retarded. In most cases, they are understaffed and operate on a shoestring budget. If there is a mental institution or retarded children's home in your area, it can provide a wide variety of opportunities for your young people to minister to some special human being who, like themselves, has been created in the image and likeness of God.

Preparation is always important when doing service projects, but especially so with a ministry to the retarded. Young people who are totally unprepared may become frightened or upset at the actions or conditions of those who are retarded. Start with a visit to the institution rather than trying to "do something" right away. A staff person from the institution can help the group with their questions and concerns.

Here are a few suggestions that any group can do with retarded persons who are residents of institutions:

1. Bring music to them. Retarded people love music with an intensity that can be surprising. A few young people with guitars or other instruments will be a hit.

2. Play games with them. Frisbee throwing, ball games, active games of all kinds are great.

3. Bring some arts and crafts projects and work on them together.

4. Talk to them. Develop a friendship with one person. Help that person with letter writing and other simple tasks that may be difficult. Go on walks with that person and take him places.

In most cases, retarded people are allowed to leave the institution as long as some responsible person is with them.

5. Provide a church service at the institution. Include a lot of singing and Bible stories.

6. Participate in a "Special Olympics." This nationally known event is conducted in local communities all over the country, and most institutions need volunteers who will be coaches, helpers, and escorts.

7. Bring a few retarded young people to your youth group meetings. You will find that they will contribute a great deal to the quality of your group.

PUPPET MINISTRY

Here's an activity that is very popular with a lot of youth groups. Develop a good puppet program, complete with a wide selection of "Muppet" style puppets, scenery, and props. There are several companies that produce puppets, scripts, recorded programs, and sound equipment. There are also seminars available that instruct kids how to do very professional puppet shows.

Once your group has both puppets and a program, take it out to underprivileged areas where there are a lot of children—the inner-city, an Indian reservation, an orphanage, or the children's hospital. Bring a fun, entertaining program with a message, and you will find that many of your young people will get very excited about this kind of ministry.

RAKE AND RUN

This is a service project that kids and the neighborhood enjoy. On a given day, all the members of the youth group gather to rake leaves. They should all bring their own leaf rakes. Load everybody into the church bus and cruise up and down streets looking for houses that obviously need to have leaves raked. One member of the group goes up to the door of the house and asks if the people desire to have their leaves raked for free. If the answer is yes, all the kids rake the lawn. With fifteen or twenty kids, it will only take five minutes to rake the leaves and bag them.

Kids should be reminded that they are on other people's property and that they should be careful not to damage anything by carelessness or horsing around. When the job is finished at each house, the kids can leave a "calling card" from the youth group that offers best wishes and lets the people know who they are. Most people are very impressed and the kids feel good about what they have done.

During the winter, this event can be called "Snow and Blow" (shoveling snow off people's sidewalks). During the spring, you could call it "Splash and Split" (washing people's windows) or "Mow and Blow" (mowing people's lawns). In each case the idea is to give an unexpected act of kindness to others.

Be sure to join us in our "Rake & Run" Party this Saturday afternoon from 1:00 until 4:00.

Bring a leaf rake (If you have one) Wear old clothes. We'll ride the bus to various deserving homes and rake their leaves and then run to the next one.

We'll eat too!

Lots of fun while we do something worthwhile for others.

SPONSOR A CHILD

There are many agencies like World Vision and Compassion International that try to find financial sponsors for children in orphanages overseas. Usually these agencies will ask for a certain amount of money to provide food, clothing, and shelter for particular children each month. Most of the time you can select a child to sponsor by name and receive detailed information about the child, including photos, and sometimes handwritten thank-you notes from the child.

Why not ask your church group to "adopt" one of these children and pledge to support the child on a monthly basis? Each person in the youth group can give a certain amount per month and/or pray for this child on a regular basis. Since the child's progress can be monitored by the entire group, the kids will feel involved in that child's life. This kind of project helps young people to develop a world awareness and a sense of compassion for others.

TRASH BASH

Collecting trash from streets and vacant lots is a community service project. A "Trash Bash" is a good way to organize and promote it with your youth group. Divide your group into teams of five or six each and assign them different areas of the community. Each person should carry a heavy duty trash bag and wear gloves. As each bag of trash is collected, it can be tied and placed in large dumpsters provided by a trash collection company.

One group turned this into a "marathon" event, with kids taking turns to work around the clock to establish a record of two hundred consecutive hours of trash collecting. Usually something like this attracts the attention of the local news media and the city officials who give the group a lot of encouragement and praise.